KATSURA

KATSURA

A Princely Retreat

PHOTOGRAPHS Takeshi Nishikawa

TEXT Akira Naito

TRANSLATION Charles S. Terry

KODANSHA INTERNATIONAL LTD.
Tokyo, New York & San Francisco

Front cover: The embossed character reads *katsura* and is taken from a letter written by Prince Toshihito.

Frontispiece: The early Katsura Palace. From a pair of six-panel screens entitled "Scenes Inside and Outside the Capital," 1615–18. Formerly owned by the Ikeda family, now in the Museum of Fine Arts, Okayama.

Note: The names of individuals before the beginning of the Meiji period, 1868, are given in the text in Japanese style—family name first.

Distributed in the United States by Kodansha International/USA Ltd. through Harper & Row, Publishers, Inc., 10 East 53rd Street, New York, New York 10022.

Published by Kodansha International Ltd., 12-21, Otowa 2-chome, Bunkyo-ku, Tokyo 112 and Kodansha International/USA, Ltd., 10 East 53rd Street, New York, New York 10022 and 44 Montgomery Street, San Francisco, California 94104. Photographs copyright ⓒ in Japan 1977 by Takeshi Nishikawa. Text copyright ⓒ in Japan by Kodansha International Ltd. All rights reserved. Printed in Japan.

LCC 75-30183
ISBN 0-87011-271-6
ISBN 4-7700-0542-3 (in Japan)

First edition, 1977
Second printing, 1982

CONTENTS

PREFACE

In 1933 the German architect Bruno Taut (1880–1938), who had fled from the Nazis the year before, arrived in Japan, where he stayed for three years. During this time he inspected several of the most important buildings remaining from the past and was moved to comment ecstatically on the Katsura Detached Palace, whose importance as a cultural monument he compared with that of the Parthenon in Athens. "An eternal thing," he called it, thus causing Japanese intellectuals of the time to reappraise a building that had to all intents and purposes been ignored for the previous century and a half.

In describing the experience of viewing the palace, Taut wrote, "In Katsura denkt das Auge"—"At Katsura the eyes think." He was struck by the simplicity of the building, by its apparent lack of ornamentation, by its just proportions, and by its spatial integration with the surrounding garden. These features seemed to him to accord perfectly with the aesthetic ideals of twentieth-century functionalism.

Yet, when one considers the Katsura Palace in the context of the Japanese architectural tradition, it is difficult to say that Taut's assessment of it was adequate. His eyes seem not merely to have thought, but to have seen at Katsura what they wanted to see, in other words a confirmation from an earlier age of the functionalist principles that Taut favored. It is true that the Katsura building—or buildings, if we include the teahouses—has less ornamentation than architecture of a similar nature in Europe, India, or China, but this is a feature that belongs to the mainstream of traditional Japanese architecture, not merely to Katsura. In his eagerness to present the palace as an example of functionalism, Taut overemphasized a more or less accidental aspect of its design. Since then, both Japanese and foreign critics have persisted in seeing the Katsura Palace as a reflection of the principles that underlie modern functionalism.

In preparing this book, we have attempted to rid ourselves of this preconceived notion and examine Katsura as it is. Our aim has been to start from scratch and arrive at an objective appraisal, which would put the palace in proper perspective with regard to Japanese architecture as a whole.

Takeshi Nishikawa spent nearly five years taking the photographs reproduced here. Visiting Katsura countless times, in all seasons and climes, he has created a realistic visual record of what he saw, making no effort to play up features that might coincide with some pet theory or creed. Of necessity, he became familiar with the *ordinary* qualities of the palace, but at the same time he looked beyond these to the brilliantly imaginative touches that set Katsura apart from other architectural monuments. His Katsura is not one that can be seen in one or two visits, but rather a total Katsura, as it might be understood by one who lived there year in and year out.

My own contribution to the book is based, first, on an actual four-year survey begun in 1961 and, second, on an examination of all the documentary sources I have been able to find over the years. From these sources, I have composed a chronological history of the Katsura Palace, to which I have added an analysis of its design from the social and cultural viewpoint. I have tried on the one hand to furnish the reader with adequate physical data and charts and on the other to point out lyrical or spiritual qualities that are not apparent from facts and figures.

Within the perimeters of traditional Japanese design, I find the Katsura Palace to be very ornamental in character, though the ornamentation is of an intellectual variety, appealing to the mind rather than to the physical senses. In scope, the creative spirit behind it encompasses not only the whole of the Japanese aristocratic tradition, but the most avant-garde ideas of its time as well. It seems to me that the Western art movement to which Katsura corresponds most closely is not functionalism, but the Mannerism of the sixteenth century.

Takeshi Nishikawa and I have attempted to show the inner spirit that led to the aesthetic philosophy of Katsura rather than the outer appearance of the buildings and the garden alone. Perhaps this is tantamount to saying that we have endeavored to show what it is about Katsura that made Taut's eyes think. If there is an eternal quality about the palace, it can only be found by the objective type of research methods that we have attempted to apply.

AKIRA NAITO
Professor of Architecture
Nagoya Institute of Technology

COLOR PLATES

5 Detail of the roof of the Imperial Gate

4 The Imperial Gate

6 The Imperial Gate viewed from inside the garden

7-8 Pebble pavement of the Imperial Pathway

9–10 Earthen wall by the Imperial Pathway

12 The Central Gate

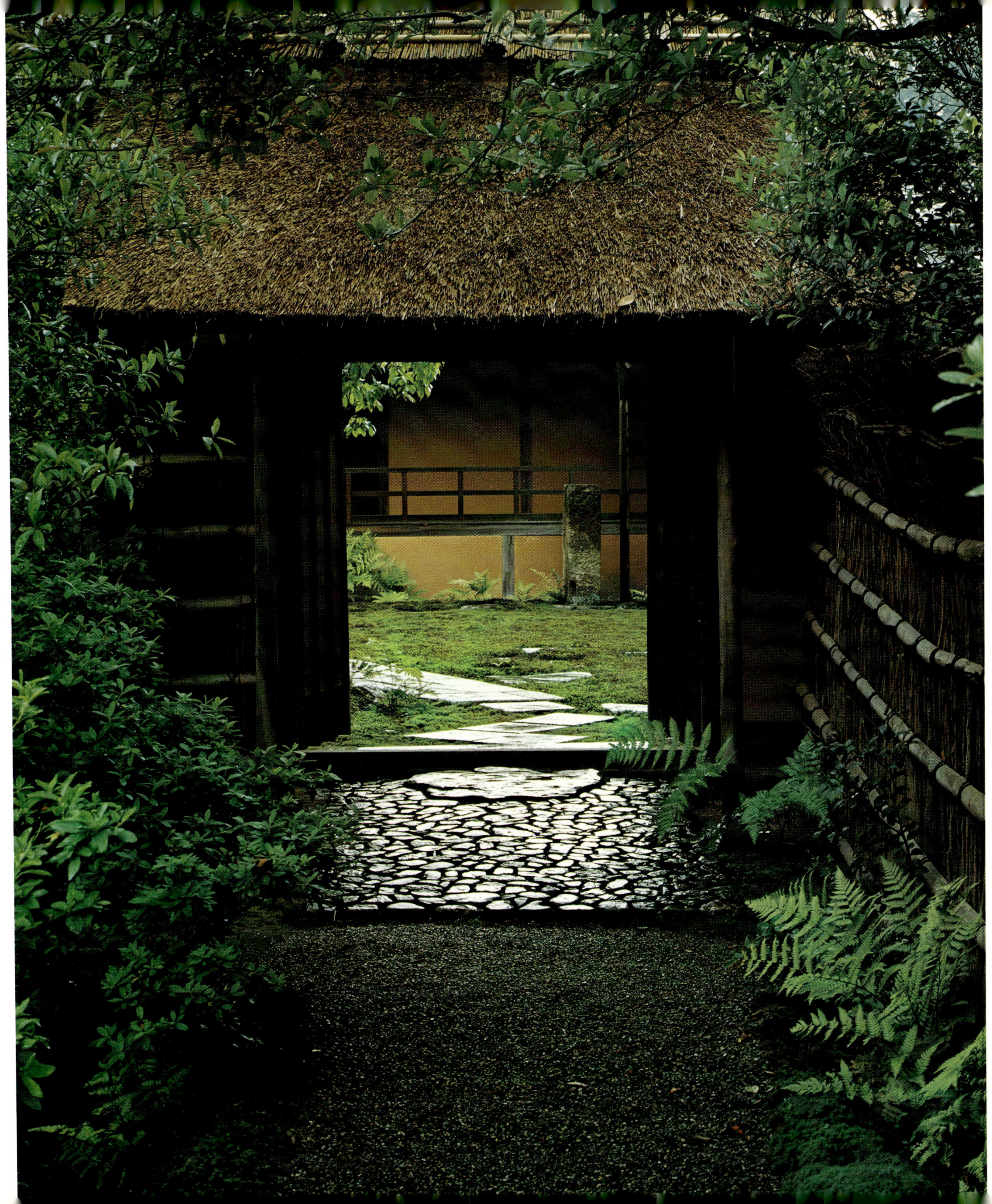

11 The Sumiyoshi Pine

13 Footpath to the Entrance Hall

14 Stone steps at the Entrance Hall

15 View of the garden from
the Second Room of the
Old Shoin

16 The pond seen in winter across the Moon-Viewing Platform

7 Tokonoma in the First Room of the Old Shoin

18 Tokonoma in the Third Room of the Middle Shoin

19 Tokonoma in the First Room of the Middle Shoin

21 The veranda south of the Music Room

22–23 Floor (left) and railing of the veranda south of the Music Room

25 Cabinets in the Dressing Room of the New Palace

27 Door fitting modeled on the character for "moon"

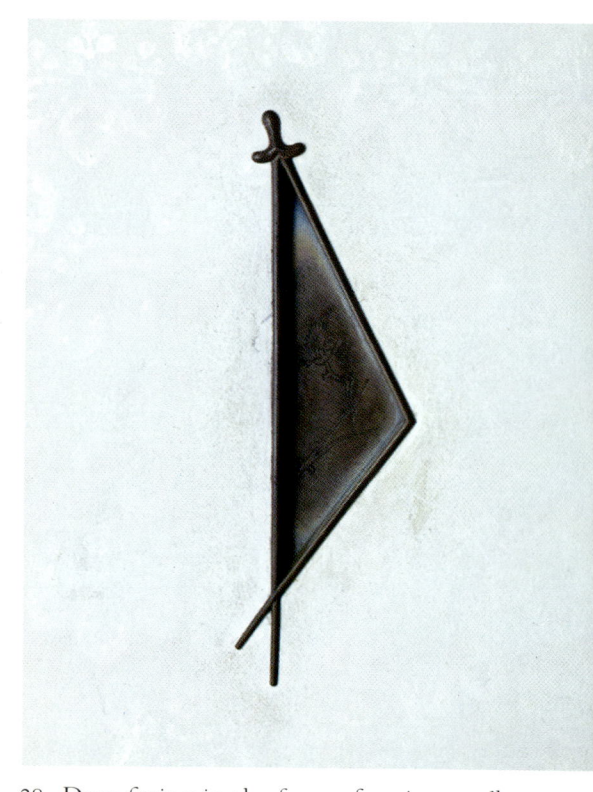

28 Door fitting in the form of a pine needle

26 Room with the Imperial Washstand

29 Door fitting in the form of a vase of flowers

30 Nail concealer in the form of a narcissus

31 The veranda of the First Room in the New Palace

32 Garden entrance seen from the garden side

33 Exit at the northeast corner of the Old Shoin

34 The main house seen from the Middle Island

43—44 Stepping stones in front of the Music Room

36–37 Stepping stones in the garden before the Middle Shoin

The south side of the Old Shoin

39–40 The main house seen from the south lawn

41–42 Drainage gutter of the Middle Shoin

46 Shoji in the late fall

45 Zigzag line of the eaves of the Music Room and the New Palace

48 The west façade of the New Palace

47 The east side of the New Palace

50 The Geppa-rō seen from the Old Shoin

51 The Geppa-rō seen from the Mount of Maples

52 Plaque in the Geppa-rō with a picture of a ship

53 The ceiling and ridge-support post in the Geppa-rō

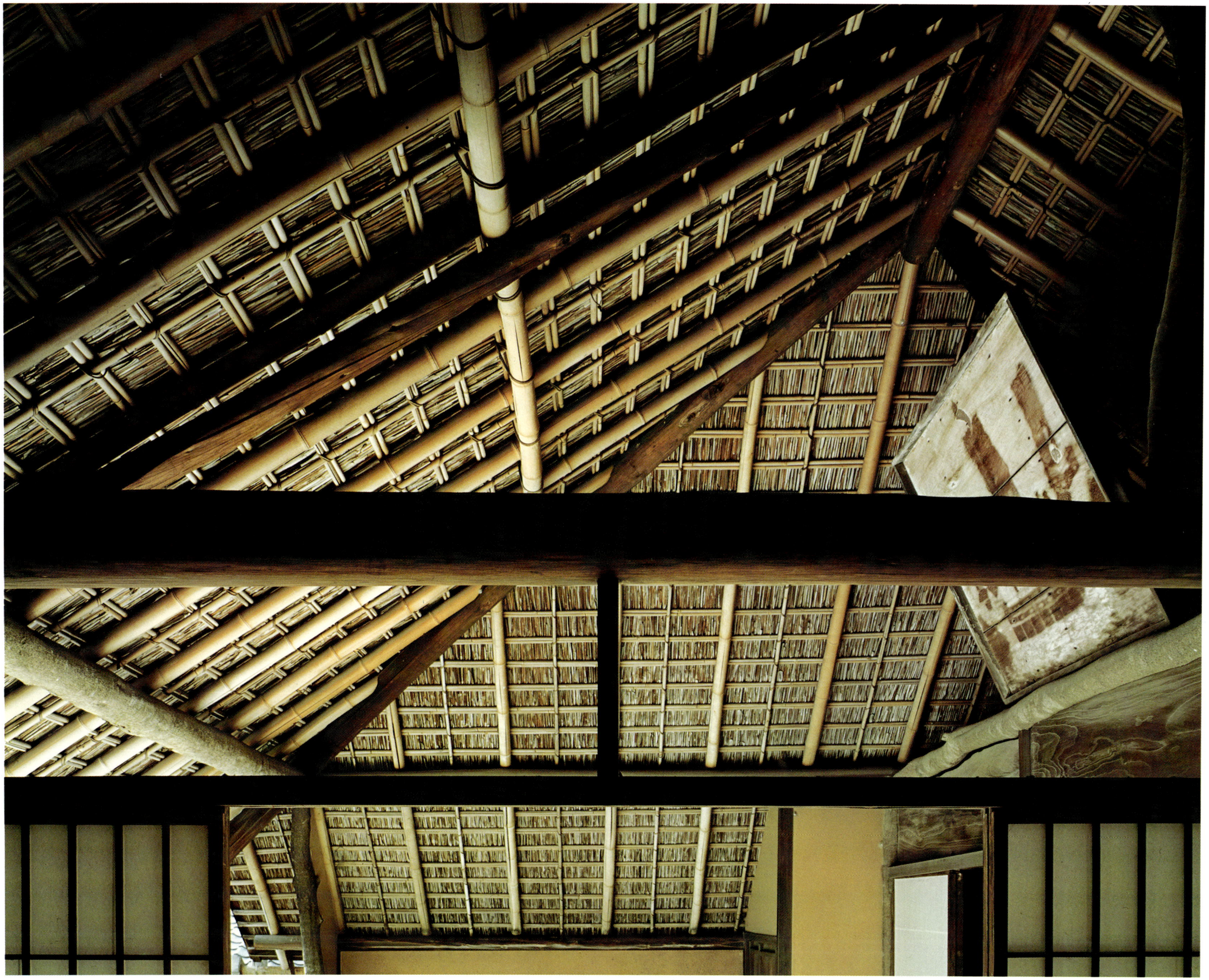

4 The ceiling in the Geppa-rō

57 The Mount of Maples

56 Amanohashidate seen from the Middle Islands

Garden bridges
seen from the
inlet before the
Shōi-ken

The Outer Arbor

60 The ceiling of the Outer Arbor

61 The wall outside the privy in the Outer Arbor

62 Water basin in front of the Outer Arbor

63 Stone walk in front of the Outer Arbor

64 Amanohashidate in the snow

Amanohashidate and the Shōkin-tei seen from the Rocky Shore

67　Stepping stones on the Rocky Shore

68 Stone lantern at the tip of the Rocky Shore

69 The northeast side of the Shōkin-te

70 Stone bridge at the Shōkin-tei

71 Front wall of the
Shōkin-tei Tearoom

72 Interior of the Shōkin-tei Tearoom

3 Rock arrangement in the pond beside the Shōkin-tei Tearoom

74 Water basin before the First Room of the Shōkin-tei

75 Amanohashidate backed by the ''Face of Night''

76 The west side of the Shōkin-

Outdoor pantry under the eaves of the Shōkin-tei

78 Amanohashidate seen from the Second Room of the Shōkin-tei

79 Tokonoma and cabinets in the First Room of the Shōkin-tei

80 The hearth and upper cabinets in the First Room of the Shōkin-tei

The Shōkin-tei seen from the southwest

Bamboo grove in the Valley of Fireflies

84 The north side of the Shōka-tei

85 Interior of the Shōka-tei seen from the west side

87 Stepping stones in front of the Onrin-dō

90 Plaque and windows under the front eaves of the Shōi-ken

91 The Middle Room of the Shōi-ken

92 Cabinets in the Third Room of the Shōi-ken

93 Pantry in the Third Room
    of the Shōi-ken

94 The thatched roof
of the Shōi-ken

KATSURA
A PRINCELY RETREAT

THE ORIGINS OF
THE KATSURA PALACE

Years of Uncertainty

Japan in the middle of the sixteenth century was still in the grip of widespread civil strife that marked the end of the medieval period. The imperial household, which had long since lost political control of the country, was in a state of extreme decline, and the Ashikaga shogunate, which had come to power two hundred years before, was no longer able to assert its authority beyond the general vicinity of the capital in Kyoto. Other regions were dominated by about twenty powerful warlords, of whom the most prominent were the Hōjō, Takeda, and Uesugi in the east and the Ōuchi and Mōri in the west. A number of the feudal barons aspired to replace the Ashikaga and establish their supremacy over the whole nation, but were too busy protecting themselves from each other to make much headway toward this greater goal. Kyoto, though largely devastated in earlier wars, was still the cultural and economic center of the realm, and it was toward the taking of this key city that the efforts of the more ambitious military leaders were directed.

A new current was being introduced into Japanese life at about this time by Europeans, who first appeared on the scene in 1543 and continued to arrive in increasing numbers for several decades thereafter. Referred to by the Japanese as Southern Barbarians (their ships came from the south), these newcomers brought with them many elements of Occidental civilization, the most important of which were European muskets and the Christian religion. Western-style firearms soon rev-

olutionized Japanese war tactics. Christianity, though later stamped out as subversive, served as a vehicle for the importation of European science, music, and art.

In 1568 Oda Nobunaga, a relatively minor baron, but one with a rich power base in the vicinity of modern Nagoya, succeeded in gaining control of Kyoto, where he proceeded to install Ashikaga Yoshiaki as a puppet shogun. Yoshiaki proved to be less tractable than expected, and in 1573 Nobunaga deposed him, thus bringing an end to the Ashikaga shogunate and simultaneously establishing himself as the leading contender for control of the nation. This date, 1573, is chosen by most historians as the beginning of Japan's early modern period.

Breaking with ancient tradition, Nobunaga took steps seemingly calculated to move the capital from Kyoto to the nearby eastern shore of Lake Biwa. There, in the area of Azuchi, he erected a seven-story castle (*Figure 1*), inspired to some extent by European, rather than Chinese or Japanese, architecture. Completed in 1579, this building was not only an impressive fortress, but a lavish palace as well—a fitting architectural symbol for the new age that was taking form around Nobunaga. Thanks partly to the latter's preferential treatment of people who chose to take up residence in Azuchi, a bustling town soon grew up around the castle moat.

By the side of Azuchi, the city of Kyoto, though much more populous, remained more sedate and better organized. There, on February 13, 1579, the Imperial Prince Toshihito, who is to be the hero of the first part of our story, was born. Named at birth Kosamaru, he was the sixth son of Prince Sanehito, himself the eldest son of the Emperor Ōgimachi.

Not long afterward, Nobunaga, who had for some time been seeking a closer connection with the imperial family, adopted an elder brother of Kosamaru, and in 1581 he urged the emperor to abdicate

1. Front elevation of Azuchi Castle, reconstructed from sixteenth-century descriptions.

from Portuguese missionaries. Weeks before he died, he established a temple, the Sōken-ji, at Azuchi and—borrowing from the native Shinto religion—erected there a stone symbolizing himself. He ordered the people to worship it and assured them that this would bring them all sorts of material and spiritual benefits. After the Christian fashion, he declared that his own birthday would henceforth be a holy day, to be celebrated annually. By this time, as the reader may infer, the culture of the Southern Barbarians had spread among the high and the low in Japan, and Christianity was exerting an important influence, if not always in the direction intended by the missionaries.

Alas for Nobunaga's pretensions, before dawn on July 1, 1582, he was set upon by a treacherous aide, Akechi Mitsuhide, at a temple called Honnō-ji in Kyoto and was either killed or driven to suicide. The Honnō-ji was burned to the ground in the course of the incident, and Nobunaga's body was never found.

Akechi Mitsuhide also killed Nobunaga's eldest son and heir, Nobutada, and set about seizing control of the country for himself. After only eleven days, however, he was attacked and killed by Hashiba (later Toyotomi) Hideyoshi, another of Nobunaga's lieutenants, who then took over Nobunaga's political authority. Such was the speed with which the political scene was apt to change in those turbulent times.

With Hideyoshi came a new age, but by no means an age of peace. It took the new dictator eight more years to subdue the warlords who had not accepted Nobunaga's rule. There were times during this interim when it seemed as though the country might revert to the chaos of the late medieval period. Because of this political instability, there was an element of uncertainty in Kosamaru's life even during his early childhood.

Hashiba Hideyoshi was a self-made man among self-made men.

in favor of the boy's father. This was obviously an attempt on Nobunaga's part to place at his own disposal the traditional authority of the emperor. Nobunaga's goal, in short, was an absolute dictatorship that would override even the imperial prerogatives. In his latter days Nobunaga seems to have decided that he was qualified to be not merely a ruler, but a god on earth, like Jesus Christ, of whom he had learned

Born of peasant stock (he did not even have a surname at first), he entered Nobunaga's army as a common foot soldier and rose to become both a brilliant general and one of Nobunaga's most highly trusted aides. Having done away with Nobunaga's assassin, he continued the struggle for unification of the country, and in 1585 he was appointed to the office of *kampaku*, or regent to the emperor. This was the highest post in the imperial government, until now invariably held by a member of the proud and ancient Fujiwara family. Hideyoshi, accordingly, arranged to be adopted by a high-ranking member of this clan. He even assumed the name Fujiwara until 1586, when, by imperial dispensation, he was given the new surname Toyotomi.* Like Nobunaga, he wished to form a closer connection with the imperial family, and to this end he adopted Prince Kosamaru, also in 1586. Around the same time, he emphasized his personal authority by constructing an enormous mansion, the Jurakudai, on the site that had once been occupied by the Imperial Palace. To enter this great establishment as Hideyoshi's adopted son was a significant turning point for the young prince, because it presumably meant that he would eventually succeed Hideyoshi as the most powerful man in the country.

A second turning point came very soon afterward, for in 1589 Hideyoshi's beloved mistress, Yodogimi, presented him with a son of his own, named Tsurumatsu. Hideyoshi, more than fifty at the time and delighted with this child of his old age, saw no further need to keep Kosamaru as his adopted heir. He therefore presented the boy with land having a substantial income of 3,000 *koku* per year** and saw to it that

he was allowed to establish a new collateral house of the imperial line. In 1590, Kosamaru became the Imperial Prince Hachijō and took up residence in a mansion north of the Imperial Palace. In this connection, it should be noted that "Imperial Prince Hachijō" is of the nature of a title, rather than a name; the young man's personal appellation became Prince Toshihito at this time.

As fate would have it, Tsurumatsu died when he was two years old, and Hideyoshi was forced in 1591 to adopt a new heir. He somewhat reluctantly chose his nephew Hidetsugu, who was allowed in the same year to succeed to the office of *kampaku*, though Hideyoshi continued to hold the reins of power. Then, in 1593, Yodogimi gave birth to a second son, called Hiroi (later Hideyori). Hideyoshi, this time seemingly demented with joy, set about dissolving his connection with Hidetsugu. Though he had dealt fairly generously with Prince Toshihito, his treatment of his nephew was cruel in the extreme. Rumors were circulated to the effect that Hidetsugu had organized a hunting expedition during the period of mourning for Emperor Ōgimachi—an unforgivable impropriety. Hidetsugu was also accused of cutting open the belly of a pregnant woman to see the child inside. There was probably no foundation for these stories, yet Hidetsugu was vulnerable, because he happened to have such a penchant for killing people, that he was known far and wide as the "Murdering Regent." The truth was that he was a general in his own right, and once he had gained a legitimate claim to succeed Hideyoshi, he was not likely to cede it to Hiroi without a struggle. Hideyoshi, for his part, was so obsessed by the desire to ensure that his lineal offspring would succeed him that he did not flinch at the most heinous methods. Ostensibly because of the deeds Hidetsugu was rumored to have done, he was banished to the Buddhist enclave on Mt. Kōya and then ordered to commit suicide. Shortly afterward, his children, along with more than thirty women in

---

* To be given a new surname by the emperor was an extremely unusual honor, bestowed on only a handful of people in the whole of Japanese history.
** A *koku* was about five bushels, the quantity of rice generally considered adequate to feed one person annually. From Hideyoshi's time until the mid-nineteenth century, land was measured in terms of the number of *koku* it yielded per annum.

his household, were dragged through the streets of Kyoto and stabbed to death on the banks of the Kamo River at Sanjō Avenue, in the shadow of a pike on which Hidetsugu's severed head was displayed.

One wonders how Prince Toshihito reacted psychologically and emotionally to this gruesome event, for only a few years earlier he had been in essentially the same position as Hidetsugu. Even though the massacre could be, and by many people was, dismissed as the aberrant act of a crazed despot, for Prince Toshihito, who was in his impressionable teens, it must have been a jolting experience—a stark revelation of the cruelty of fate and the violence of the times. The young prince must have felt himself helplessly caught in a racing current, uncertain where it would take him. In the following period, the current was to remain strong, but the prince's destination was eventually determined. At that point the history of the Katsura Palace began.

Edo and Kyoto

In the 1590s two movements were under way that presaged the coming of a new era. One took place in Kyoto, the other in Edo.

Eight hundred years had elapsed since the Emperor Kammu (reigned 781–806) established his capital in Yamashiro Province and named it Heian-kyō, "the capital of peace and tranquillity." The city was originally laid out on a nearly square grid plan, adapted from that of the Chinese capitals at Ch'ang-an and Lo-yang. Nine broad avenues ran from east to west and eight from north to south, plus a wide boulevard extending from the imperial inner city at north center to the main gate of the city at south center. The large squares of the grid were subdivided by smaller streets into blocks, which in turn were broken up into lots for houses. In general, the plan reflected the ancient Chinese tradition that the emperor should sit at north center and his subjects face him from the south. There is no proof that the plan for Heian-kyō, or Kyoto as we call it today, was ever fully implemented; there may have been large vacant areas from the beginning. Furthermore, much of the city was laid waste during the wars of the middle ages. Still, the concept of Kyoto as an imperial metropolis, the hub of the nation's cultural and economic activity, remained alive until the late sixteenth century. All this changed with the rise of Nobunaga and Hideyoshi, who, with utter disregard for tradition, proceeded to destroy much of what remained from the past and rebuild the city in a fashion that suited themselves. In the process, the resplendent Heian-kyō of the imperial age became, to all intents and purposes, a large castle town.* The construction work entailed in this transformation was in full swing in 1590.

As we have seen, Hideyoshi chose the ancient palace ground as the site for his own domicile, the Jurakudai, which was surrounded by a moat and in many respects resembled a castle. The moat was circled by a zone for the houses of various daimyo and generals. The emperor, along with his courtiers, was moved to what had been the northeast corner of the original city plan. This area came to be called "Nobility Town." Numerous temples that had been scattered about the city were relocated in areas known as "Temple Towns." There were two of these, north and south, but a few of the oldest and most prestigious temples were left where they were. Still other districts were marked off for

* "Castle town" (*jōka-machi*) as used here distinguishes a city that grew up in the vicinity of the castle of a feudal lord from other types of cities that developed during the premodern age, such as port towns or towns that took form around famous temples. Castle towns normally had fairly distinct zones for the houses of warriors, the houses or shops of ordinary townspeople, temples, and so on.

commoners, which is to say merchants and artisans. In effect, then, the city was redivided along class lines: a quarter for warriors, another for the emperor and the nobility, another for temples, and another for ordinary townspeople. At the same time, the street system was partially restored and to some extent revised, and the whole urban area was surrounded by a protective embankment, about 22.5 kilometers in perimeter and roughly oval in shape. This enclosure extended from Mount Takagamine on the north to Kujō Avenue on the south and from the Kamo River on the east to the Kamiya River on the west (*Figure 2*). That which was within this fortification was regarded as being in the city (*rakuchū*), and that which was not, out of the city (*rakugai*). The Kyoto that we know today developed from Hideyoshi's castle town, rather than directly from the original capital, Heian-kyō.

Also in 1590, Tokugawa Ieyasu, one of Hideyoshi's most powerful generals, began work on his castle in Edo. After Hideyoshi died of illness in 1598, Ieyasu defeated the supporters of his heir at the battle of Sekigahara in 1600 and in 1603 was appointed shogun. At this point, Edo, the seat of the shogun's government, replaced Kyoto as the center of political authority. Henceforward, Nihombashi, the "Bridge of Japan," which was in the heart of Edo's most flourishing commercial district, became the point from which all distances were reckoned. From here extended a new pattern of national control marked by a radial system of roads. The main arteries were the Five Great Highways (*Figure 3*): the Tōkaidō, leading down the Pacific coast to Kyoto; the Nakasendō, leading down through central Japan to Kyoto; the Nikkō Kaidō, leading north to the Tokugawa mausoleum in Nikkō; the Kōshū Kaidō, leading west into the provinces of Kai and Shinano (present-day Yamanashi and Nagano prefectures); and the Ōshū Kaidō, leading to the provinces of the northeast (Fukushima and Miyagi prefectures).

2. Kyoto and its surroundings in the early Tokugawa period. The plan of Heian-kyō is superimposed.

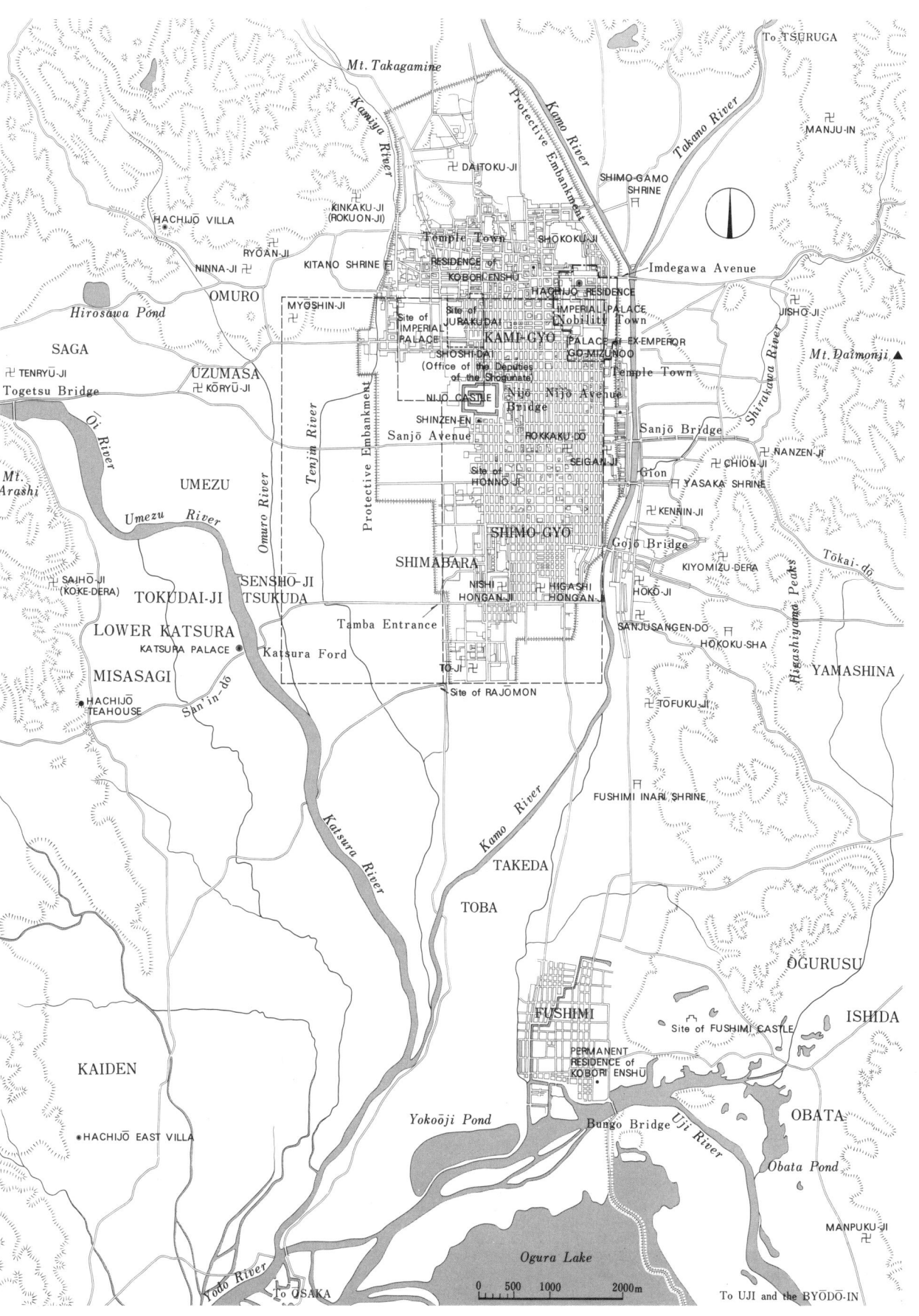

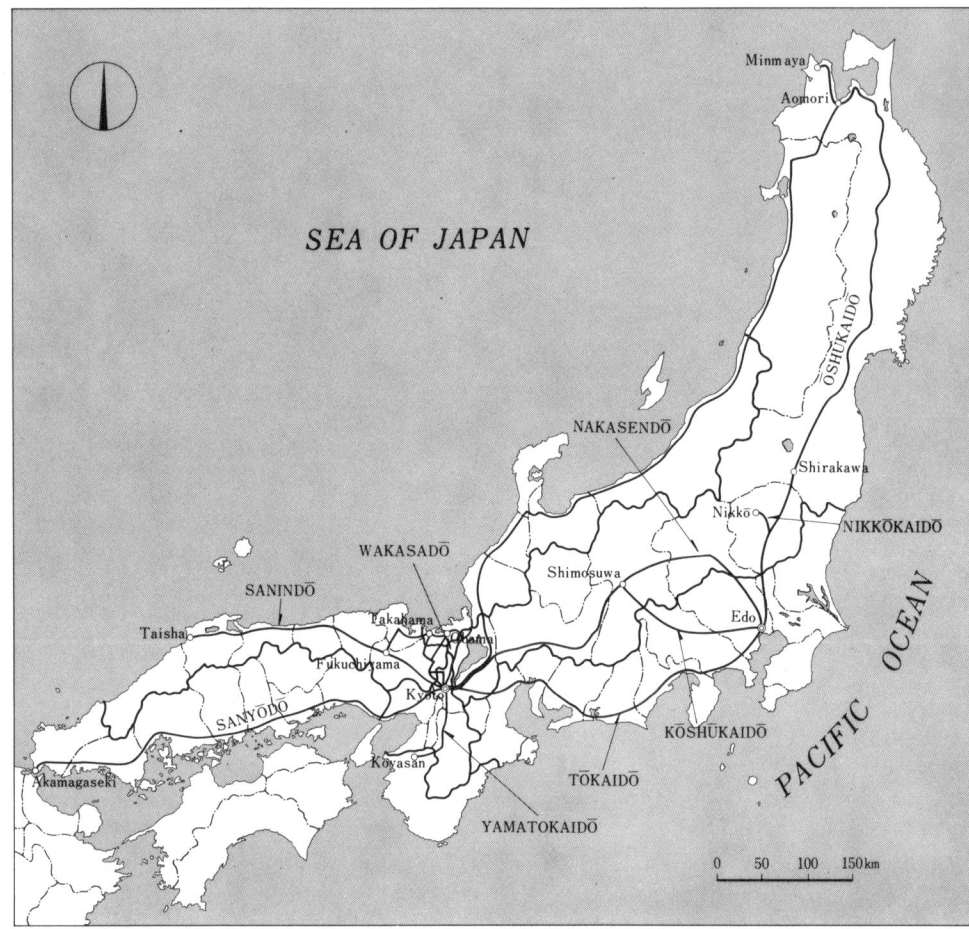

3. The Five Great Highways radiating from Edo, the seat of the Tokugawa shoguns.

In earlier times, the country was divided into seven areas called "routes," all linked to Kyoto by highroads. The Tōkaidō was one of these, but only a secondary one. After 1603, it became the most important thoroughfare of all, and its orientation was reversed—Edo was now the front end, and Kyoto the back end. So far as politics were concerned, after 1603 the back followed where the front led. To the

emperor, as well as to noblemen like Prince Toshihito, this must have been a galling situation, for they, after all, were the possessors of a cultural heritage that stretched back into ancient times. From the orthodox Chinese viewpoint on which the imperial government had originally been founded, they were the rightful rulers. Whether they approved or disapproved of the shogunate, however, during the Edo period (1603–1868), they were unable to move without its concurrence.

As though symbolizing their subjection, Kyoto became oriented toward the east, rather than the south, as Heian-kyō had been. The city was now dominated neither by the Imperial Palace nor by the Jurakudai (this was dismantled in 1595, when Hideyoshi moved to Fushimi Castle), but by Nijō Castle, constructed by Tokugawa Ieyasu somewhat farther to the south. The main entrance of this fortress was on the east side, and the street directly approaching it, Nijō Avenue, accordingly ran from east to west. If one went straight down this thoroughfare from the castle to the eastern side of the city, then south for a short distance and east again, one arrived at Sanjō Bridge, which was the entrance to the Tōkaidō and consequently the new main gateway to the city. It follows that the "back door" to Kyoto was on the west side. This was the Tamba Entrance, which marked the beginning of the San'indō, the ancient highway leading toward the Inland Sea. The village of Katsura, where the Katsura Palace is situated, was about three kilometers beyond the Tamba Entrance.

On the western side of Kyoto, there is a river originating in the mountains to the northwest and flowing down past the city to link with the Kamo River at a point to the south. This stream is known by a number of names, depending on the section being referred to. In its upper reaches, where there is a famous series of rapids, it is called the Hozu River. Below a dam at Mount Arashi, it becomes the Ōi River, then the Umezu River, then the Katsura River. At the point where it is traversed by the San'indō, it is the Katsura River, and the place where travelers crossed it was called Katsura Ford. If we consider the Sanjō Bridge on the east as the gateway for those in Kyoto who truckled to the government in Edo, we may consider Katsura Ford as the exit for those who turned their backs on the shogunate. The Katsura Palace is just north of the old ford on the opposite side of the river from Kyoto.

Katsura Village

The question of when the Katsura Palace was first built devolves upon that of when the village of Katsura came into the possession of Prince Toshihito, and the answer to this is conjectural. In 1590, when the prince was allowed to establish the house of Hachijō, Hideyoshi, as noted above, gave him a grant of land, but this land comprised the three villages of Ishida, Ogurusu, and Kobata, which are some distance south, not west, of Kyoto. Only eleven days before Hideyoshi died, he replaced this bequest with a new allotment of nine villages in Tamba Province representing the same income. The reason for the transfer is not clear, but unless Hideyoshi changed the grant again in the last eleven days of his life, which seems unlikely, Prince Toshihito had no connection with the village of Katsura during Hideyoshi's lifetime. As we shall see, this is a point of some importance, because it refutes one of the misleading legends concerning the origins of Katsura Palace.

The death of Hideyoshi in 1598 threw the political scene into confusion, for Hideyoshi's heir, Hideyori, was still only a small child and could not himself govern the nation. It soon became apparent that Tokugawa Ieyasu intended to rule in his stead, and the feudal lords split into two large factions, the Eastern Army supporting Ieyasu and the Western Army backing Hideyori's claims. This was the confrontation that led to the battle of Sekigahara in 1600, in which Ieyasu won a decisive victory. Ieyasu immediately confiscated lands belonging to his enemies and redistributed them to his allies, so that the political map was completely changed. Hideyori, who had had no direct part in the battle, was allowed to retain his base at Osaka Castle, together with the provinces of Settsu, Kawachi, and Izumi (present-day Osaka metropolitan area), but his total holdings were sharply reduced, from 2,000,000 *koku* to 650,000 *koku*. He still had the support of a number of daimyo, as well as that of tens of thousands of displaced samurai whose lords had lost their status after Sekigahara, but the combined forces behind him were not strong enough to prevent Ieyasu from assuming control, as was clearly demonstrated by the appointment of Ieyasu as shogun in 1603.

In 1605, Ieyasu passed the office of shogun on to his son Hidetada and ostensibly retired. The principal purpose of this move was to make the shogunate hereditary in the Tokugawa family, and even after his resignation, Ieyasu continued to exercise control from his castle at Suruga (present-day Shizuoka). Hideyori, now reduced to the position of one daimyo among many, was forced to pledge fealty to the house of Tokugawa, which for its part imposed strict surveillance on the activities of the Toyotomi faction. The shogunate also exacted obedience from the emperor and his court, who in any case were dependent upon it for their subsistence.

By way of demonstrating that the Tokugawa government was to be permanent, the shogunate carried out an extensive reconstruction program at the Imperial Palace, in the course of which the area occupied by the court nobles was redivided and rezoned. At this time, Prince Toshihito's mansion was moved to a site north of the palace, where it faced Imadegawa Avenue on the north. This seems to have

4. Scene showing the Summer Siege of Osaka Castle, from a pair of six-panel screens entitled "The Battles of Osaka" (*Osakajin-zu Byōbu*), c. 1620. Osaka Castle Office.

occurred around 1605. It is likely that the nine villages in Tamba Province bestowed on the prince by Hideyoshi were replaced by the area around Katsura at about the same time.

The first tangible proof that the village of Katsura belonged to the house of Hachijō is a certificate of ownership issued on October 10, 1617, under the seal of Tokugawa Hidetada. Two years earlier, the Tokugawa armies had completely destroyed the Toyotomi in the famous Winter and Summer Sieges of Osaka Castle (*Figure 4*), and one year earlier Tokugawa Ieyasu had died. The document in question, therefore, may be regarded as a reaffirmation by Hidetada of his father's bequests to Prince Toshihito. The grant stated, in sum, that six villages—Senshō-ji and Tsukuda on the east bank of the Katsura River and Tokudai-ji, Misasagi, Kaiden, and Lower Katsura on the west bank—were to belong to the house of Hachijō "just as in the past." The last phrase may be taken as corroboration of the theory that these areas, which lie on either side of Katsura River, became the property of Prince Toshihito at the time when his residence in Kyoto was moved, particularly since it would have been normal for a new shogun to confirm or revise such land allotments at the time of his accession, which in Hidetada's case was 1605. We shall make no great mistake, therefore, in assuming that the Katsura Palace could not have been in existence earlier than this year.

The "Little Teahouse in the Melon Patch"

On May 9, 1611, Emperor Go-Yōzei ceded the throne to his third son, seventeen-year-old Prince Korehito, who thereupon became the Emperor Go-Mizunoo (also called Go-Minō). Originally, Go-Yōzei had wanted to name Prince Toshihito, who was his younger brother, as his successor, but this idea was dropped because of anticipated opposition from the shogunate. The Tokugawa, after all, could not be expected to favor as emperor a man who had once been the adopted son of Toyotomi Hideyoshi, however brief the period of adoption. The situation might have been different a few years later, but in 1611, it will be recalled, Toyotomi Hideyori was still alive and was regarded by Ieyasu as a dangerous rival. In any case, elimination from the imperial succession may be considered the third turning point in Prince Toshihito's life.

In 1613, only two years after the accession of Go-Mizunoo, Tokugawa interference in the affairs of the emperor and the court became more intense and more explicit with the issuance of the five-article Rules for the Nobility (*Kugeshū Hatto*). These regulations enjoined the nobility to "follow the path of learning and the arts" and tacitly forbade them to engage in political activity.

The final destruction of the Toyotomi, which came on June 4, 1615, led to the fourth turning point in Prince Toshihito's life. The suicide of Hideyori at Osaka Castle made a widow of his wife, the Lady Sen, who was a daughter of Tokugawa Hidetada. The marriage had been a political one in the first place, arranged just before Hideyoshi's death for the purpose of cementing relations between the Toyotomi and the Tokugawa, and now the Tokugawa saw a new use for the bereaved lady. In January or February, 1616, they suggested that she be betrothed to Prince Toshihito. Because of the death shortly afterward of Ieyasu, the chief proponent of this match, the plan was never carried out, but the incident symbolizes the role of subservience to which Prince Toshihito was reduced, while also making it clear that Ieyasu considered the prince important enough to be the husband of his granddaughter.

5. The members of an excursion to the Katsura area are entertained by dancers (center left) in this detail from a pair of six-panel screens entitled "Scenes Inside and Outside the Capital," early seventeenth century. Collection of Hiroaki Banno.

Possibly to escape momentarily from the political manipulations of the shogunate and the court, on July 20, 1616, Prince Toshihito went to Senshō-ji Village "to view his melons" and later "took a walk," as the documentary source puts it, along the Katsura River. He took with him a group of noblemen, poets, and dancers, and this is good reason to think that the "walk" was a very festive outing—a momentary opening of the clouds that darkened the prince's sky (*Figure 5*). Two days later, the consort of the ex-Emperor Go-Yōzei made a "progress" to the village of Katsura, and it is only reasonable to suppose that suitable facilities for entertaining her existed there—at least a teahouse or some similar building. The record of this visit is the earliest suggestion of the country house that was to become the Katsura Palace.*

* References to both excursions appear in the *Years of Prince Toshihito* (*Toshihito Shinnō Gonenreki*). This book was compiled in the mid Edo period and includes some of the prince's diaries.

93

In December, 1616, or January, 1617, Prince Toshihito married the daughter of Kyōgoku Takatomo, Lord of Tango Castle. At the time, the prince was thirty-seven, and we may regard the marriage as the fifth and final turning point of his life, because in many ways it signified his taking an independent, neutral stand between the court and the Tokugawa government. The Kyōgoku were of the military class, but were relatively close to the imperial court. By allying himself with them through marriage, the prince could demonstrate that he was not blindly loyal to the nobility, but at the same time not so completely dominated by the Tokugawa as he might have been had he married the Lady Sen.

In the spring of 1617, the prince made his first visit to Edo. Since his house had been established with the assistance of the Toyotomi, he had frequently visited Osaka Castle, but now, despite his own sense of independence, it was necessary to pay tribute to the Tokugawa shogun at Edo Castle. One supposes that the prince's real purpose was to sound out the shogun's attitude toward him, and that he felt the trip to be vital to his future.

Though it was an age in which the shogunate was constantly impressing its authority on the emperor and the court, the shogun, Hidetada, received Prince Toshihito with remarkable cordiality, and it would appear that the two men discussed means of relaxing the emotional tensions that existed between the Tokugawa government and the nobility. It may even be that they conferred on a plan dear to the heart of the Tokugawa, namely the marriage of Tokugawa Kazuko, another of Hidetada's daughters, to the emperor. Shortly after this, in the summer of 1617, Hidetada paid his first visit to Kyoto since the death of his father. No doubt, one of his aims was simply to assess any political changes that may have resulted from Ieyasu's death, but his principal purpose was to pursue the proposal for Kazuko's betrothal.

By marrying Kazuko to the emperor, the Tokugawa would create a familial link with the imperial household, and once the marriage was accomplished, there was little doubt but that Kazuko would be named empress.* Gossips had been speculating on the marriage since the time of Kazuko's birth in 1608, and for very good reason, because throughout Japanese history, the holders of true political power had invariably taken steps to form this sort of relationship between themselves and the emperor. Only recently, there had been the precedent of Nobunaga's adopting Prince Toshihito's brother and Hideyoshi's adopting the prince himself (it might be noted that both were brothers of the heir apparent to the throne). The first actual move on the part of the Tokugawa had come in May, 1614, when Tokugawa Ieyasu discussed the possibility of Kazuko's betrothal with an imperial envoy at Suruga. The negotiations had been interrupted by the siege of Osaka Castle and then by Ieyasu's death.

The prospective bridegroom, who was the future Emperor Go-Mizunoo, was not disposed to look upon the shogunate's proposal with favor. He regarded it as sheer insolence. Even so, by 1618 it was virtually certain that the marriage would take place. The shogunate was consequently both shocked and vexed in that year to discover that, unbeknown to them, the emperor had had an affair with the daughter of a nobleman named Yotsutsuji Kintō, and that this lady had now produced a son, Prince Kamo. The Tokugawa government laid aside for a time its plans for Kazuko, but took steps to punish the courtiers considered responsible for allowing the emperor to commit this "immoral act." Three high members of the nobility were banished to distant areas, and a number of others were forbidden to appear at court.

* The emperor had numerous consorts from among whom the empress was selected. The importance of the empress's position was that her children had priority of succession among the emperor's offspring.

In a letter that seems to have been written on August 23, 1618,* Prince Toshihito mentions discussing this matter with Konoe Nobuhiro and Yotsutsuji Suetsugu—the elder brother of the emperor's clandestine lady, who herself was known as Oyotsu—at the "little teahouse in the melon patch in Lower Katsura." This reference, together with the record of the visit of Go-Yōzei's consort to Katsura in the summer of 1616, strongly suggests that by 1616, the year of his marriage, Prince Toshihito had at least built the earliest version of the Katsura Palace. It remains for us to conjecture what sort of an establishment this "little teahouse in the melon patch" was.

The First Country House at Katsura

Two principal historical sources indicate what the earliest version of the Katsura Palace was like. The first is a screen painting that has been handed down in the Ikeda family, the rulers of the Okayama fief. Like many other sixteenth- or seventeenth-century works showing panoramas of the Kyoto area, it is entitled "Scenes Inside and Outside the Capital" (*Rakuchū Rakugai-zu Byōbu*). It consists of two six-panel screens and was painted sometime between August, 1615, and January, 1618.

The second source is a writing, dated 1625 and entitled *Record of the Katsura Pavilion* (*Katsura-tei-ki*), by the monk Sūden of the Konchi-in, a subtemple of the Nanzen-ji in Kyoto. The author tells of having been invited to Katsura by Prince Toshihito and relates his impression of the place. Sūden, it should be noted, was a Tokugawa minion who

* The month and day are clear, but the year does not appear in the message. A variety of related circumstances suggest that the letter was composed in 1618.

6. The early Katsura Palace. From a pair of six-panel screens entitled "Scenes Inside and Outside the Capital," 1615–18. Formerly owned by the Ikeda family, now in the Museum of Fine Arts, Okayama.

wielded such power in Kyoto that he was spoken of as the "Black-Robed Premier." The first source is particularly important because it is visual, but Sūden's written description furnishes a valuable clarification of the scene appearing in the screen painting.

In the Ikeda family's "Scenes Inside and Outside the Capital," the Katsura Palace is depicted in the upper left-hand corner of the left screen (*Figure 6*). In this screen, the south is to the left and the north to the right. Consequently, the river flowing into the garden from the upper right and descending to the lower left can be taken to represent a branch of the Katsura River that started somewhere north of the garden and flowed through it to the south. In terms of the present-day Katsura Palace, this stream must have entered the compound at about the point where the Ordinary Gate is, flowed past the guardhouse, then under the bridge at the end of the Imperial Pathway, then south of the Mount of Maples and southwest of the teahouse called Shōkin-tei to the lower end of the garden. It seems that the designer of the garden utilized a natural riverbed along which the Katsura River, or a part of it, had flowed at one time or another. The river has frequently shifted its course slightly.

To the right of the strand under the bridge crossing the upper part of the stream, another rivulet appears to enter the garden. According to Sūden's *Record of the Katsura Pavilion*, there were indeed two streams, and it would seem that this second course corresponds to the one that now flows by the arrangement called Amanohashidate toward the north side of the Shōkin-tei. The two rivulets must have flowed together to form a pond at a point near the middle of the present-day pond. In earlier times, the pond had no large islands such as those that exist today, but there were islets that may be regarded as prototypes. On the left (south) side of the picture, near the point where the river flows out of the garden, there was a second bridge. Its location seems to have been about the same as the present boat mooring southwest of the Shōkin-tei. On the whole, it seems that the pond was originally positioned more to the northeast, which is to say closer to the Katsura River, than it is today.

It appears that there was at first a sort of levee along the pond to protect the grounds at times when the Katsura River flooded. Traces of such an embankment still exist, and something that corresponds to it can be made out in the screen painting. Judging from Sūden's

description, a distinction was drawn between the inner and outer gardens. The inner garden was to the southwest of the pond, where the houses were situated, and the outer garden was to the northeast. Visitors from Kyoto, after crossing the Katsura Ford, would arrive at the outer garden. The main gate, which was to the east of the present Shōkin-tei, is shown in the Ikeda family's screen painting as a low thatched-roof structure (at the center of Figure 6), through which a number of people who appear to be samurai and merchants are passing. From the gate, the inner garden was approached by way of the lower bridge. If one walked around the pond past the south side of the main house, one came to the upper bridge, which led back into the outer garden. At this point there was a row of shrubbery broken by a small gate with a grass-thatched roof. Just beyond, in the outer garden, was a kiosk, also with grass thatch. This was a teahouse, and in the screen painting there is a person inside in the dress of a tea-master. Behind the kiosk the painting shows a number of maple trees, from which it may be assumed that this area corresponded to what is now known as the Maple Riding Lane, below the Mount of Maples. On the riverbank in front of the kiosk is a large pine tree; this is probably the once famed Takasago Pine, which no longer exists.

Sūden referred to the buildings at Katsura with such Chinese-sounding terms as "golden pavilion," "flower palace," and "jeweled tower." Some scholars have taken these words literally and assumed that the early Katsura Palace was a luxurious Momoyama-style mansion, but in fact Sūden's composition was of the nature of a eulogy, and the extravagant terminology he employed is mere rhetoric. The fancy words occur for the most part in the first section of his account, in which he is being shown into the compound. In the middle section of his work, the descriptions are more matter-of-fact and consequently more reliable. It is difficult to suppose that Prince Toshihito had the resources to build a great mansion to use merely as a country house, and we may assume that the earliest buildings at Katsura were similar to those in the screen painting.

In the central area, the illustration shows a house with a thatched main roof and projecting auxiliary eaves covered with cypress-bark shingles. On the left, connected with the first building in zigzag fashion, is a second house with a boarded roof. It is clear from the composition of the painting that these are the principal buildings. We may suppose that the one on the right is the more important of the two, for we can see inside it two people in long-sleeved kimonos, who appear to be noblemen. On the east side is a large stepping stone leading into the garden. In its less florid passages, the *Record of the Katsura Pavilion* speaks of the house as a "mountain cabin" and says that from it one could see, to the east, Mount Hiei and the peaks of Higashiyama; to the west, Mount Arashi; and to the north, the Ryōan-ji (the temple famous for its rock-and-sand garden) and the heights of Takagamine. It must be assumed from Sūden's description of the view that there were no large trees blocking the garden off from the outside as there are today.

The house with the thatched roof seems to have stood about where the annex containing the Entrance Hall is today, and the building with the boarded roof occupied approximately the same site as the present Old Shoin, though it is to be noted that the boarded-roof house in this picture is different in style from the Old Shoin. Standing prominently in front of the houses in the picture is a plum tree. This adds to the credibility of the painting, because Prince Toshihito is known to have been particularly fond of plum trees. In this liking, he followed the Emperor Go-Toba (1180–1239), whom he greatly admired. Go-Toba, we may note, was not only an outstanding patron of literature—he compiled the *New Anthology of Ancient and Modern Poetry* (*Shin Kokin Wakashū*) and gathered around him such outstanding literary figures as Fujiwara no Sadaie and Kamo no Chōmei—but also something of a hero to noblemen of later times because of his efforts to overthrow the Kamakura shogunate.

All in all, it appears that the Katsura country house constructed by Prince Toshihito was considerably more modest in scale than the present Katsura Palace. "Little teahouse in the melon patch" is not too wide of the mark.

Katsura Palace after the Marriage of Kazuko

The marriage of Tokugawa Kazuko to the Emperor Go-Mizunoo finally took place on July 17, 1620, amid unprecedented pomp and splendor. On the same day, construction work of some sort was begun at the Katsura Palace. Opinions differ as to what was done, but it seems likely that the work principally concerned the garden, rather than the house. One suspects that Prince Toshihito, who had been active behind the scenes in arranging the emperor's marriage, was so happy to see it carried off satisfactorily that he decided to celebrate by spending some money on his country home.

After Kazuko's marriage, the prince became more active in public affairs. In August, 1623, when Tokugawa Iemitsu took office as the third shogun in the Tokugawa line, Toshihito acted as representative of the emperor at the appointment ceremonies.* Then, in April, 1625, he

* When a shogun succeeded to his office, he was given the official appointment by the emperor. This was strictly a matter of form, because the emperor had no power to withhold the nomination. Still, the practice preserved the fiction that the shogun was the emperor's servant.

made his second trip to Edo, where he was lavishly entertained by Iemitsu and his subordinates. Nothing like this had happened during the time of Ieyasu, who apparently was unable to forget the connection between Prince Toshihito and the Toyotomi family and was consequently inclined to regard the prince as an enemy. In this age when the lives of the nobility were strictly regulated by the shogunate, Prince Toshihito was quite exceptional. His 3,000-*koku* estate was small in comparison with the holdings of the feudal lords, but it represents far more wealth than most members of the nobility had. Moreover, to be able to build a country house—even a "little teahouse in the melon patch"—set the prince apart from others of his class.

As Prince Toshihito assumed a greater role in public life, visitors came more frequently to the Katsura Palace. One caller was the priest Kinshuku Kentaku of the Shōkoku-ji, who spent a day at Katsura in July, 1624, and wrote that it had "the finest view in Japan." Another visitor was Sūden, who saw the palace in July, 1625, and composed the *Record of the Katsura Pavilion*, mentioned above. In general, the people whom Prince Toshihito invited to his country place were among the leading cultural figures of the age. It is no exaggeration to say that Katsura Palace and its garden were by this time becoming a cultural focal point, as well as the symbol of a cultural epoch in Kyoto.

Prince Toshihito fell ill in April, 1629, and died on May 29 at the age of fifty. His lifetime coincided with an era of sudden and violent change, but he had somehow survived the political upheavals and contributed to the establishment of harmony between the imperial court and the shogunate. But for chance, he might well have become Hideyoshi's heir or, later, emperor. Yet today he is known primarily for his broad cultural interests. The history of the early Katsura Palace came to an end with his death.

THE LATER KATSURA PALACE

Decline of the Early Katsura Palace

The period of good will between the shogunate and the imperial court following the marriage of Kazuko to the emperor was short, less than a decade.

The Emperor Go-Mizunoo, infuriated by the shogunate's direct and indirect meddling, angrily resigned on December 22, 1629, in favor of his daughter by Kazuko. Princess Okiko became the Empress Meijō. The emperor's move was so sudden that neither the Empress Kazuko nor the *kampaku*, Ichijō Kanetō, knew about it in advance. Meijō, whose formal accession was celebrated in October, 1630, was the first woman to occupy the throne since the Empress Shōtoku in the eighth century. Since she was the daughter of Kazuko, Tokugawa Hidetada was the new empress's maternal grandfather, and the ruling shogun, Iemitsu, was her uncle. With her succession, therefore, relations between the court and the shogunate entered a new stage, in which the shogun could deal with the imperial family as blood relatives.

The new attitude of the shogunate toward the nobility is implicit in a comment on the abdicated emperor written some years later by Hayashi Razan, a Confucian scholar serving the shogun: "Alas, the proud boy [the emperor] is disobedient to his father [the shogun], and there is nothing to be done about it. In past years, the military class has attempted to be good to the court, but this is apparently impossible."

Prince Toshihito's son and heir was born on December 9, 1619, and was given the name Takomaro. Early in 1627, the boy was renamed Imperial Prince Noritada (also called Toshitada) and appointed the second head of the house of Hachijō. His early years were spent, then, in the time of Tokugawa Iemitsu, which in many ways was the golden age of the Tokugawa shogunate. As it turned out, one result of the Tokugawa government's paternal attitude toward the court was that the history of the Katsura Palace entered a new phase.

After the death of Prince Toshihito in 1629, the country house at Katsura was allowed to run down badly. The priest Kentaku of the Shōkoku-ji, who had visited the place several times during the prince's lifetime, stopped there again in September, 1631, and was appalled at its condition. In his diary, *Rokuon Nichiroku*, he wrote: "Since the death of Keikō-in [*i.e.*, Prince Toshihito], there have been no repairs, and everything has deteriorated. I was greatly distressed. I recalled the past with great affection."

No doubt much damage was caused by natural calamities, which occurred frequently in this area around this time. Records show that there were numerous earthquakes in 1629, and on October 13, 1632, the region suffered what was described as "the worst typhoon in thirty years." In September the next year, another typhoon flooded the Yodo River Valley, and it is certain that the Katsura River overflowed at this time. There must have been very little that the young Prince Noritada could do to prevent the country house, which he had inherited from his father, from falling into a state of disrepair.

Reconstruction of the Palace

In September, 1632, Prince Noritada made his first trip to Edo, where he was received by Iemitsu on September 15. The prince was one of a party of nobles who had come to pay respects to the shogun on the first anniversary since Hidetada's death of Ieyasu's original entry into Edo.* Noritada was only thirteen at the time, and the underlying purpose of his presence was probably to demonstrate that the house of Hachijō still retained an important position in the court at Kyoto. At a banquet held four days later in the main hall at Edo Castle, Iemitsu gave the prince a parting gift of one thousand pieces of silver and thirty kimonos.

In August, 1634, Iemitsu paid a formal visit to Kyoto, accompanied by a retinue of no fewer than 307,000 persons, including numerous daimyo. The shogun was entertained on a grand scale by imperial commissioners, representatives of the ex-emperor, noblemen, and prelates alike. He utilized the occasion to smooth relations between the shogunate and the court. To this end, he increased the ex-Emperor Go-Mizunoo's landholdings from 3,000 *koku* to 10,000 *koku*, made other grants to various noblemen, and even distributed a liberal quantity of silver to the people of Kyoto. Go-Mizunoo, for his part, informally offered Iemitsu the exalted position of grand chancellor in the imperial government.** Iemitsu refused, thus cleverly making a show of modesty before the imperial court while at the same time demonstrating that he was above it all. Though peace between the court and the shogunate was Iemitsu's principal aim, he also wished to display the

solid power of the shogunate and the seeming inexhaustibility of its financial resources. The trip was a huge success in many ways, but the ex-emperor's basic attitude of resistance toward the shogunate did not change, nor was the shogun's determination to control the court in all important matters lessened. In a sense, Iemitsu was simply showing the ex-emperor and the court that from now on he would treat them as children.

Curiously enough, the shogunate's self-confidence led it to attempt to ape the imperial court in numerous respects, but Edo's efforts to incorporate the culture of the nobility into that of the relatively uncouth warrior class frequently ended only in ostentation on the latter's part. Tokugawa Iemitsu spent vast amounts of money in an effort to satisfy his cultural vanity. Immediately after his trip to Kyoto, he started building a spectacular mausoleum for Ieyasu at Nikkō. The result was the extremely gaudy Tōshō-gū, which may be regarded as Iemitsu's first and last direct contribution to the nation's cultural heritage (*Figure 7*).

Yet it was also Tokugawa Iemitsu's money that made possible the rebuilding of the Katsura Palace, for the shogun seems not only to have given Prince Noritada a substantial amount of gold around 1640, but also to have made more or less regular contributions to him in later years.

In October, 1642, Prince Noritada married Ofū, the daughter of Lord Maeda Toshitsune of Kaga (present-day Ishikawa Prefecture). This was a marriage of convenience, in the sense that it was convenient for the shogunate, and Iemitsu sent the prince a betrothal present of three hundred pieces of silver and fifty bolts of cloth. To make Lord Maeda's daughter more presentable socially, it was arranged that she would be adopted before her marriage by the Empress Dowager Kazuko, who was now called Tōfukumon-in. This marriage is merely one more

---

* Tokugawa Ieyasu first entered Edo in 1590, on the first day of the eighth month, according to the lunar calendar in use at the time. Throughout the Tokugawa period, the anniversary of this date, called *hassaku*, was one of the most important family celebrations of the Tokugawa. The date on which Prince Noritada was received was the second of the eighth month, the day after *hassaku*.

** Though the real power was in Edo, the centuries-old imperial bureaucracy continued to exist. It had virtually no authority over anything save itself, and even here its decisions were subject to the shogun's approval. Still, titles in the imperial hierarchy were highly coveted by members of the military class.

7. The Tōshō-gū at Nikko, erected in honor of Tokugawa Ieyasu, whose remains were carried here in 1617. The Karamon ("Chinese Gate") at center opens onto the oratory and main hall.

example of the shogunate exercising its authority over the personal lives of the nobility. Still, for those who regard the Katsura Palace as the crystallization of the aristocratic tradition of Kyoto, it is a sobering truth that the reconstruction of the palace around the time of Noritada's marriage was carried out largely with Tokugawa money, just as the construction of the Tōshō-gū had been.

The Old Shoin and the Middle Shoin

The main house is the only part of the present Katsura Palace thought to have been built before Prince Noritada's marriage. It is focused around a section known as the Middle Shoin (*Figure 8*).

The name *shoin* refers to a house in the *shoin-zukuri*, or simply *shoin*, style, which was the norm for upper-class Japanese residences after about the end of the fifteenth century. The typical house in this style was partitioned into a number of rooms, of which the most important had a window with a sill broad enough to be used as a desk (this was called a *shoin* window); an alcove (*tokonoma*) where a flower arrangement or an art object, or both, could be displayed; and a set of staggered shelves (*chigaidana*) for books or ornaments. This architectural form evolved over two or three hundred years beginning in the thirteenth century.* In the case of the Katsura Palace, *shoin* refers to several distinct sections of the main house, each of which has a *shoin* room.

According to the *Record of the Country House at Katsura* (*Katsura Gobetsugyō-no-ki*),** the paintings on the doors and wall panels in the First Room of the Middle Shoin were by Kanō Tan'yū; those in the Second Room by Kanō Naonobu; and those in the Third

* There is much room for confusion of terms, for the word *shoin*, literally "book room," was originally used only in reference to a study found in the houses of Zen Buddhist abbots, but in later times it came to designate any house having such a room. The study room was adopted into the houses of the rich, where it came to be used not as a study but as a room for receiving guests. It grew in size and grandeur until in the larger mansions it became an enormous audience hall (*hiroma*).
** The family that acted as stewards to the house of Hachijō produced this document around 1804. The original manuscript has been lost, but several later versions of the *Record of the Country House at Katsura* have been handed down. The one now in the archives of the National Diet Library, Tokyo, is accepted by scholars as the most reliable and is the one referred to here.

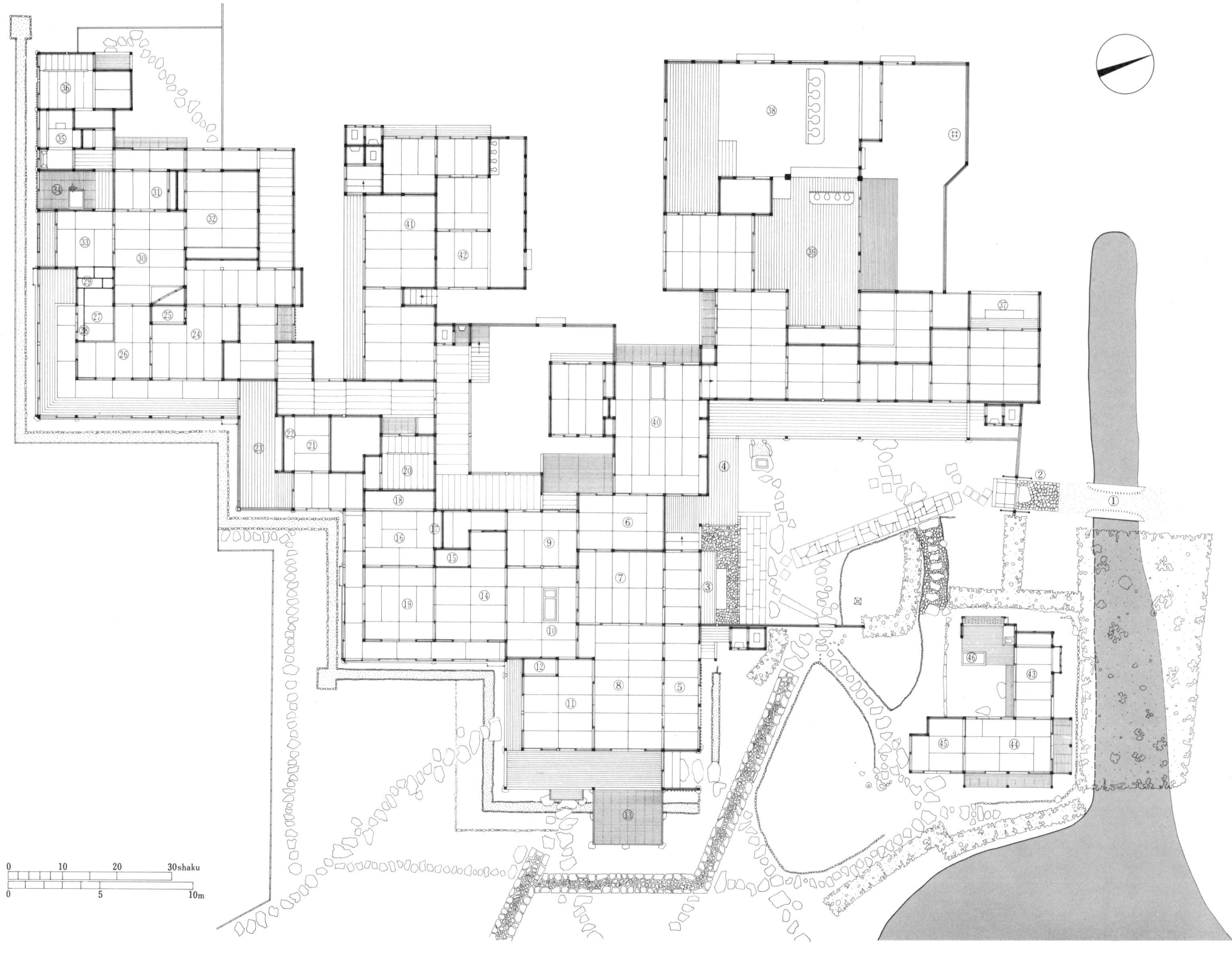

8. Plan of the main house, the Geppa-rō, and surroundings (mid Edo period).

1. Earth-covered bridge
2. Central Gate

Old Shoin
3. Entrance Hall
4. Tiger Veranda
5. Veranda with tatami
6. Pantry
7. Spear Room
8. Second Room

9. Auxiliary Room
10. Hearth Room
11. First Room
12. Tokonoma in the First Room
13. Moon-Viewing Platform

Middle Shoin
14. Third Room
15. Tokonoma in the Third Room
16. First Room

17. Shelves
18. Tokonoma in the First Room
19. Second Room
20. Bathroom

Music Room
21. Music Room
22. Tokonoma in the Music Room
23. Veranda of the Music Room

New Palace
24. Second Room
25. Tokonoma in the Second Room
26. First Room
27. Imperial Dais
28. *Shoin* window
29. Katsura shelving
30. Imperial Bedroom
31. Closet

32. Room for Sleeping
33. Dressing Room
34. Room with the Imperial Washstand
35. Lavatory
36. Bathroom

Service Wing
37. Service entrance
38. Dirt-floored room
39. Kitchen

40. Servants' quarters
41. Servants' quarters
42. Kitchen

Geppa-rō
43. First Room
44. Middle Room
45. Auxiliary Room
46. Hearth

Room by Kanō Yasunobu. A comparative study of the style of these paintings and other known works by the same artists confirms the authenticity of the Katsura paintings.

The three Kanō brothers were very much in demand both at the imperial court and at Edo Castle. From a variety of sources, it can be deduced that the only time when their services would have been available simultaneously at Katsura was the first half of the year 1641. Consequently, it would appear that the Middle Shoin was constructed at that time.

Just after his marriage, Prince Noritada is known to have gone to Katsura for a lengthy stay, and one must therefore suppose that by then the country house was rather commodious. A consideration of the Middle Shoin confirms this assumption, for the building is of a type that would normally have been used for the master's personal quarters in a larger house. This apartment would have been incomplete without the Old Shoin on the east to serve as a place for receiving guests and the so-called Music Room on the west as an area for the prince's wife. From the functional viewpoint, it would also have required a kitchen, as well as rooms for ladies-in-waiting and servants. There is every reason to suppose, therefore, that all, or nearly all, of these various sections of the main building were completed in 1641, when the Middle Shoin was built, or at the latest by the time of Prince Noritada's marriage in 1642.

An examination of the architecture with respect to style indicates that the Old Shoin, as its name indicates, predates the Middle Shoin. There are clear traces of reconstruction beneath the roof and floor, from which it can be inferred that the building was moved sometime after its original construction and attached to the Middle Shoin. One may conclude that the Old Shoin was a part of the original "small house in the melon patch," and that the Middle Shoin was added on later.

The Five Teahouses

Construction work continued at the palace after the marriage of Prince Noritada. Since the main house from the Music Room eastward was already complete, it may be assumed that later efforts centered on the garden and the teahouses scattered about in it.

In the summer of 1645, Prince Noritada made his second trip to Edo, where he was received by Iemitsu and Iemitsu's youthful heir, Ietsuna. It seems likely that the prince reported to the shogun on the reconstruction work at Katsura and requested further financial aid from him. Around the same time, we find Prince Noritada traveling to a number of districts and looking at famous teahouses. In Sakai (present-day Osaka), for example, he made a thorough inspection of teahouses designed by Sen no Rikyū, which may well have given him a number of hints later incorporated into the Shōkin-tei. By 1647 at the latest, the Katsura garden had been improved to the extent that the prince could not only hold tea parties there in the daytime, but also extend invitations to his friends for such nocturnal pastimes as watching the moon rise or boating on the pond to see the distant lights of the surrounding villages.

From a writing by a Zen priest who visited Katsura in the summer of 1649, we learn that at that time there were five teahouses in the garden. Today there are four teahouses: the Geppa-rō, the Shōkin-tei, the Shōka-tei, and the Shōi-ken. A fifth, called the Chikurin-tei, formerly existed, but has now disappeared. Since the historical sources available mention no teahouses other than these five, it is assumed that they are identical with those mentioned by the Zen priest. In this connection, it should be noted that two other small buildings now standing in the garden—the Outer Arbor and the Arbor for Four—are not teahouses, but shelters where guests may rest while waiting to be served.

Let us now consider the teahouses one by one. Geppa-rō means "Moon-Wave Tower"; the name comes from a poem by Po Chü-i (772–846) about the reflection of the moon shimmering in the rippling waters of a lake. In order to present a similar view at Katsura, the building was placed on an artificial two-meter eminence overlooking the pond. This is why it is called a tower (rō), even though the building itself is only one story high.

According to the *Record of the Country House at Katsura*, the Geppa-rō was built in the time of Prince Toshihito and was at first known as the "Plum Teahouse" or the "Moon-Plum Teahouse." To judge from the Ikeda family's "Scenes Inside and Outside the Capital," however, the building did not exist in Prince Toshihito's time, for on the site corresponding to its present location, we find only a large plum tree (*see Figure 6, page 95*). Furthermore, it cannot be supposed that a hillock and teahouse would have been placed directly east of the main house, where they would block the view of the pond.* The Geppa-rō must, therefore, have been built after the reconstruction and expansion of the main house in the early 1640s; most likely it was set up three or four years later by Prince Noritada, who may well have given it the alternate name "Plum Teahouse" in commemoration of the plum tree his father had loved so.

From an architectural viewpoint, the interior space of the Geppa-rō is splendid. The building is only fifteen by twenty-four feet in area, but the treatment of the roof structure and ceiling is such that there is a remarkable atmosphere of spaciousness. The ceiling is of the *keshō-yaneura*, or "decorated roof-underside," type; the beams, rafters, and lathing are exposed, but made of more ornamental materials than would normally be used. Ceilings of this kind are often found in

* It will be recalled that the main house in the screen painting was northwest of the present Old Shoin.

9. The Middle Room of the Geppa-rō. The plaque on the north wall reads "Gekka" "Song of the Moon."

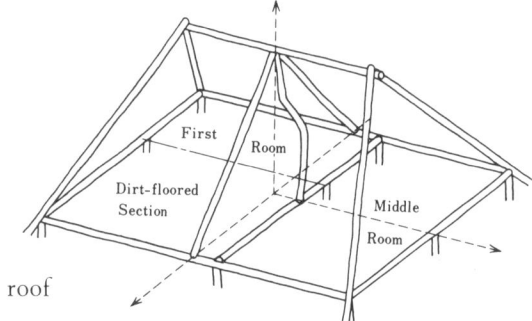

10. Rough diagram of the Geppa-rō roof structure.

tearooms or teahouses. The roof is supported by an unusual structure based on the principle of the balancing-man toy. Four slanting beams rise from the corners of the building, and the ridge pole, which is placed longitudinally, is further supported by a curving king post resting on a tie beam (*Figures 9 and 10*). The result is perhaps the richest spatial effect to be found in the entire Katsura Palace.

The Shōkin-tei, or "Pine-Lute Pavilion," is situated directly across the pond from the Geppa-rō and forms a good pair with it—whereas the Geppa-rō looks down on the water from a high position, the Shōkin-tei hugs the ground not far above water level. If we consider the Geppa-rō, along with the Old Shoin and the Middle Shoin, as representative of the sunny, active side of the Katsura Palace, then the Shōkin-tei may be described as the shady, inactive side. In the earlier version of the Katsura Palace that we know from the Ikeda family's screen painting, the site of the Shōkin-tei was at the point where visitors entering through the main gate got their first view of the pond. It was from the boat mooring southwest of the Shōkin-tei that a bridge led across the lower part of the pond to the inner compound. When the main house was reconstructed and enlarged, the pond was extended to the southwest, and part of the former inner compound was converted into the Middle Islands. With these improvements, the grounds took on, to a much greater extent than before, the aspects of a tour garden, as opposed to a view garden.* It can be surmised that Prince Noritada built the Shōkin-tei to serve a purpose similar to that of the grass-thatched kiosk in the outer compound of the earlier palace.

* These are the two principal types of Japanese gardens. The tour garden is usually spacious and, as the name implies, is intended to be walked through. As a rule, the garden path meanders past a succession of striking settings, often arranged to suggest historical locales or famous scenic spots, such as Amanohashidate, a celebrated sandbar on the coast of the Sea of Japan, which inspired a section of the Katsura garden. The view garden, which at times is very tiny, is intended to be admired from the interior of the house.

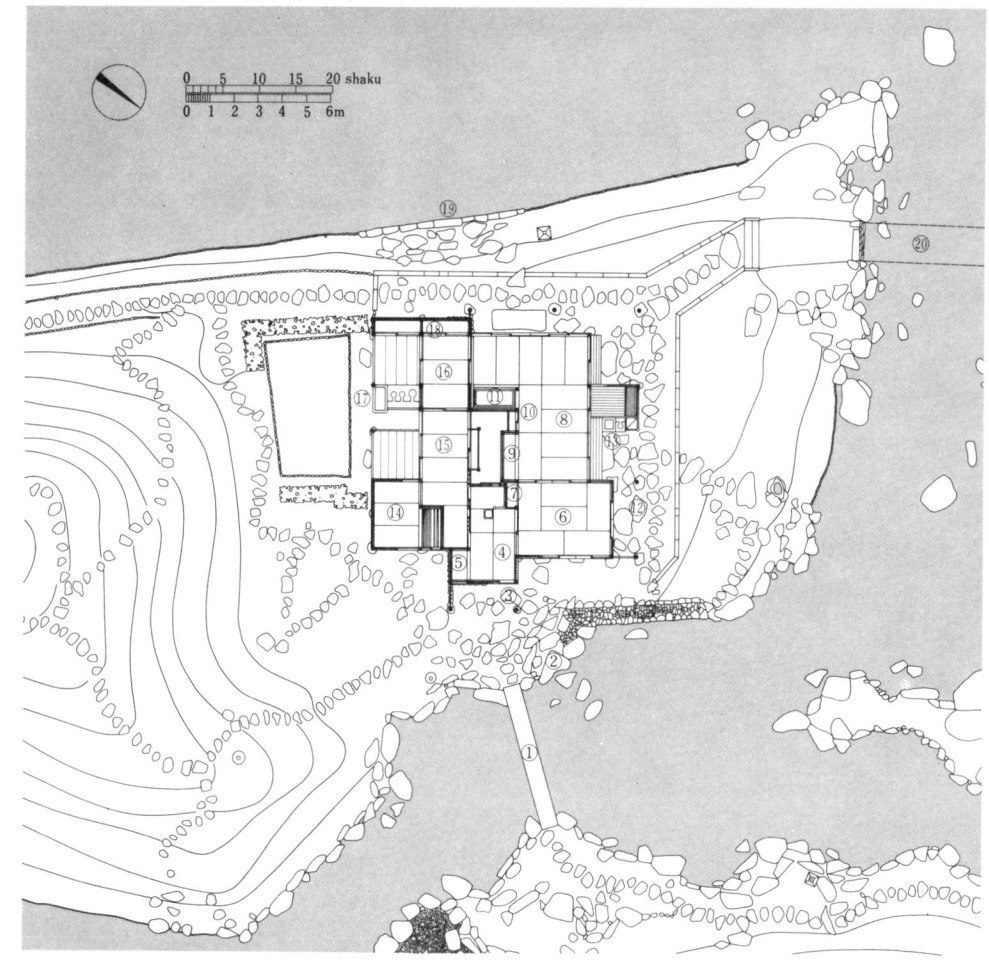

11. Plan of the Shōkin-tei and surroundings (mid Edo period).

1. Stone bridge	7. Cabinets	14. Pantry
2. Place to wash hands in running water	8. First Room	15. Back Room
3. Entrance to the Tearoom	9. Tokonoma in the First Room	16. Auxiliary Room
4. Tearoom	10. Closet	17. Hearth
5. Tokonoma in the Tearoom	11. Hearth	18. Cabinets
6. Second Room	12. Unfloored loggia	19. Boat mooring
	13. Hearth	20. Site of red-lacquered bridge

The most unusual element in the design of the Shōkin-tei is the unfloored loggia (*tsuchibisashi*) on the west side facing the pond (*Figure 11*). In the middle of this there is a sort of open pantry (*mizuya*) used for preparing the tea ceremony implements and washing them afterward. This would normally be at the back of the house, where it would not be in full view of the tea drinkers. The extended eaves of the loggia are supported by three oak logs, left in their natural state. There is, on the whole, a certain roughness in the design here which is not to be found in the other teahouses, and this feature, taken together with the fact that the roof is thatched, strongly corroborates the idea that the design was made with the rustic kiosk of Prince Toshihito's time in mind.

Because of this similarity to the teahouse in the screen painting, many have concluded that the Shōkin-tei was actually built in Prince Toshihito's day. The best documentary evidence for this theory is found, again, in the *Record of the Country House at Katsura*. It states that the plaque reading Shōkin ("Pine-Lute"), now hanging under the northeast gable of the building, was written by the Emperor Go-Yōzei, who was Prince Toshihito's elder brother. There is no way of being certain, however, that this plaque was originally intended for this building. This theory is consequently dubious.

Actually, in determining the age of the Shōkin-tei, the most pertinent evidence is the fact that the paintings on certain door panels on the cabinets above the hearth in the First Room are by Kanō Tan'yū. For a number of reasons, he could not have worked at the Katsura Palace at any time other than the year 1641. Another clue as to the age of the building is found in the heavy papering used on the walls of the tokonoma and on the sliding doors between the First and Second Rooms of the teahouse. The vivid blue-and-white checkered pattern dyed into this paper is so unusual and so colorful that it has long since

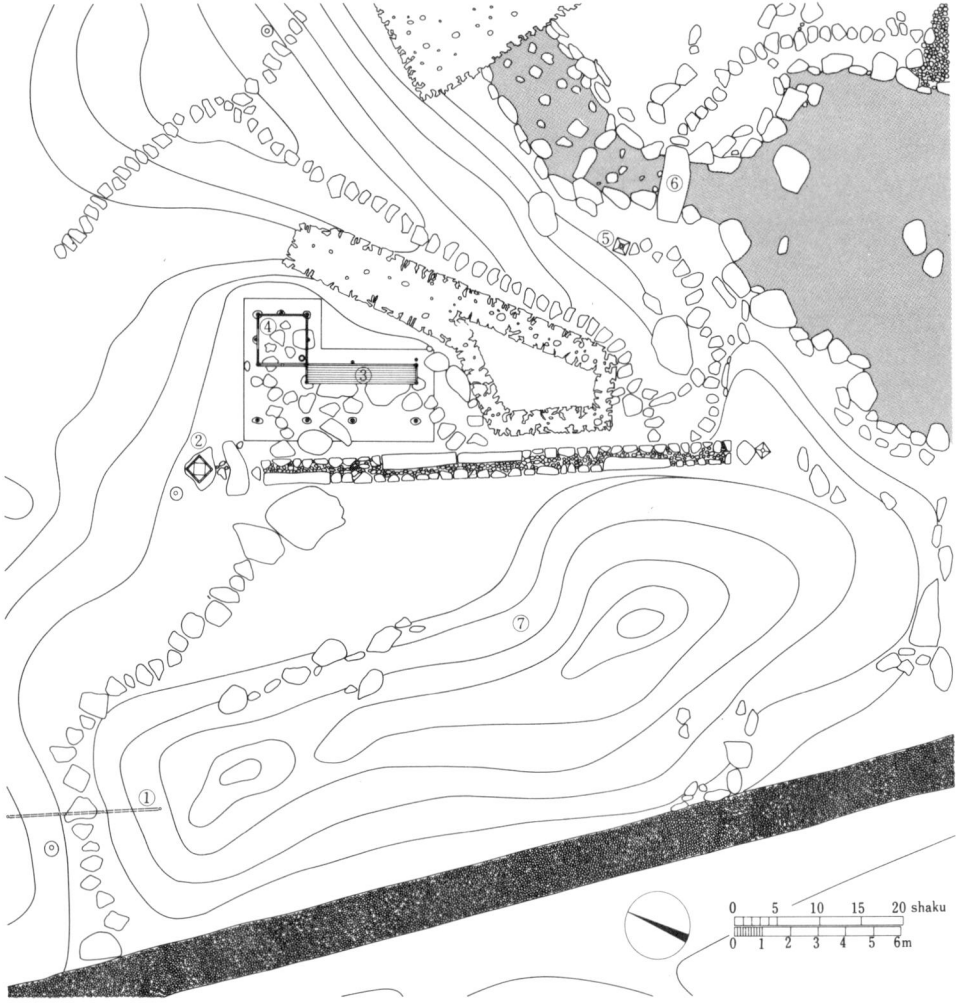

12. Plan of the Outer Arbor and surroundings (mid Edo period).

1. Site of gate with a hedge fence
2. Water basin
3. Bench in the Outer Arbor
4. Privy in the Outer Arbor
5. Oribe-style lantern
6. Stone bridge to the Rocky Shore
7. Fern palms

become a symbol of the Shōkin-tei, and it is difficult to believe that this particular adornment was not a part of the original design. Moreover, the paper itself is of an especially fine variety that was made in Kaga Province. It would be most natural to suppose that the paper was designed and produced around the time of Prince Noritada's marriage to the daughter of the Lord of Kaga.

Nevertheless, there are obvious reasons for considering that the Shōkin-tei as it now stands was built in installments. In the first place, the shingled roof of the Tearoom on the back of the building cuts very awkwardly into the thatched roof on the front side—too awkwardly to suppose that the juncture of the roofs was part of the original plan. Moreover, the facilities in the open pantry at the front are duplicated in the back, which would not have been necessary if there had been a single overall plan. Apart from the building itself, there is the question of the approach: at present, visitors arrive on the northeast side of the building by way of a stone-slab bridge, traditionally thought to have been contributed by Lord Katō Yoshiaki of Aizu-Wakamatsu, a contemporary of Prince Toshihito, but in the past there was a bridge with red-lacquered railings that led from the edge of the pond on the west side of the building to a point near the strand known as Amanohashidate. The accepted rules for the design of tour gardens permit only one main route through a garden (though spurs are allowed), and it seems unlikely that there would have been two paths here, particularly when the presence of two conspicuous bridges in the small corner devoted to Amanohashidate would have cluttered the design of an otherwise generously spaced garden.

It would appear, therefore, that the Shōkin-tei was built in at least two stages. Most likely, the section with the thatched roof was erected around the time of Prince Noritada's marriage, and the Tearoom with the shingled roof added afterward, though no later than 1647. In this

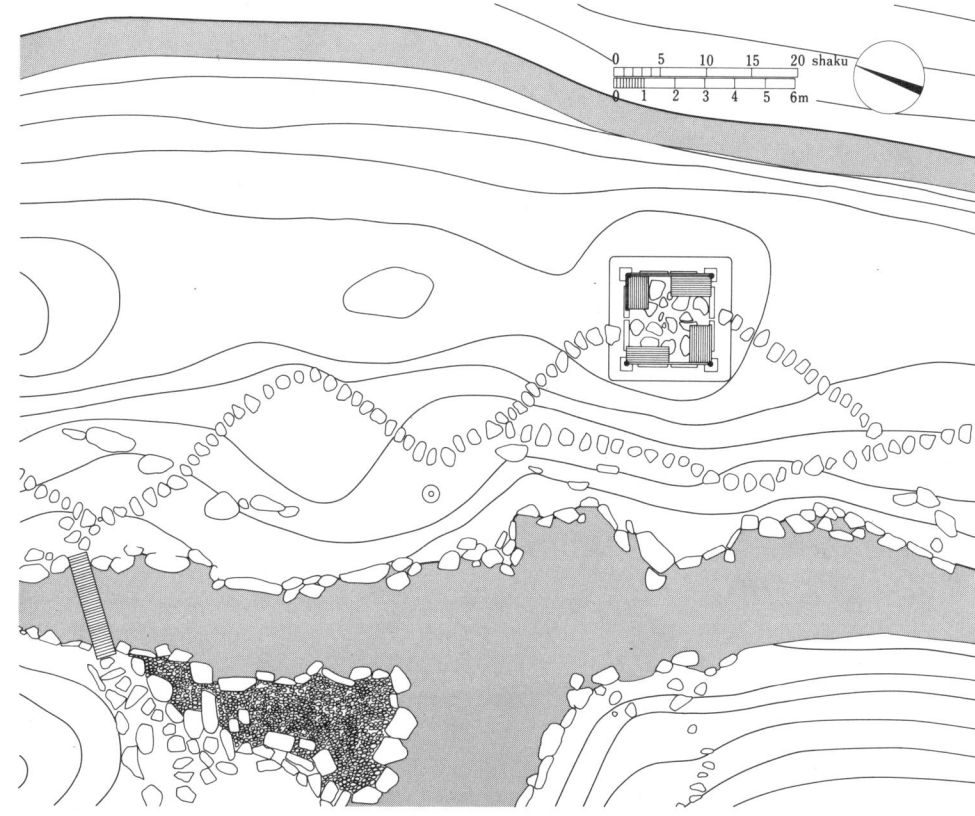

13. Plan of the Arbor for Four and surroundings (mid Edo period).

case, the building would have originally been approached from the Maple Riding Lane by way of the bridge with the red railings, which was presumably removed when the stone-slab bridge was installed. It may be assumed that the Outer Arbor and the Arbor for Four (*Figures 12 and 13*), both of which are subsidiary to the Shōkin-tei, were built at about the same time as the section with the shingled roof.

After leaving the Shōkin-tei, one walks south, turns right—crossing the earth-covered bridge over the Valley of Fireflies—and then starts up a "mountain path." At the top of the rise is a small teahouse called

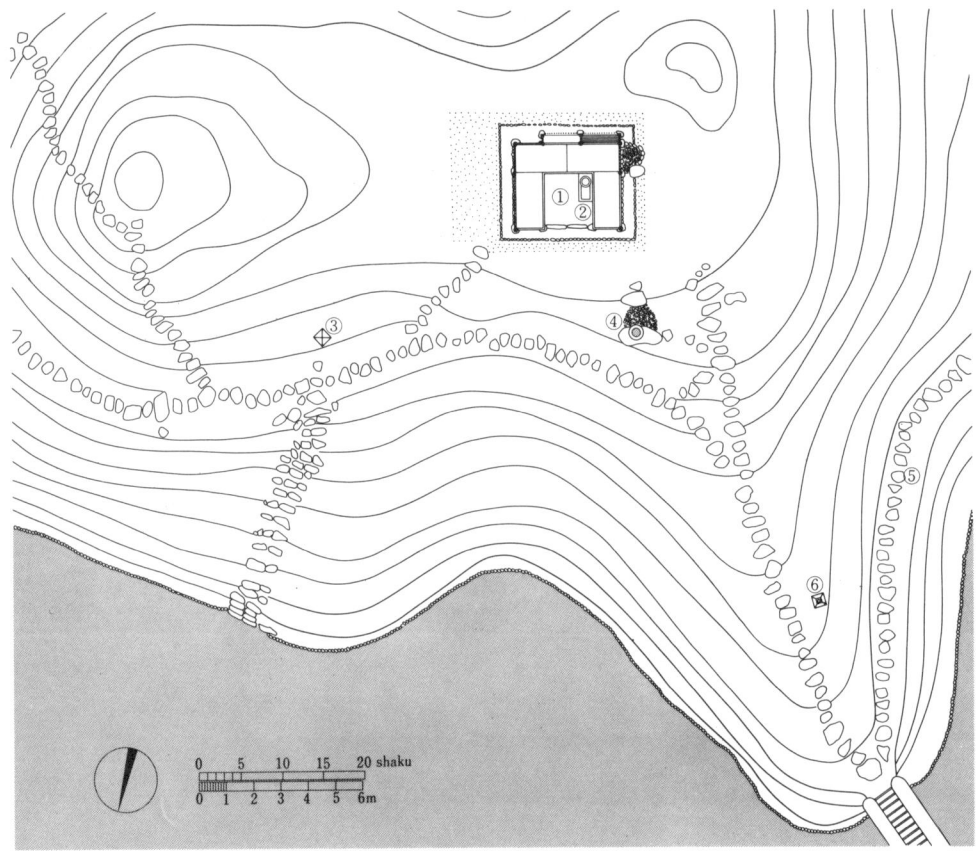

14. Plan of the Shōka-tei and surroundings (mid Edo period).

1. Dirt-floored section
2. Hearth
3. Firefly Lantern
4. Water basin
5. Path leading to the Onrin-dō
6. Oribe-style lantern

the Shōka-tei. Its location is the highest point in the garden and the first along the main route from which one has a complete view of the main house, albeit through the trees. The hillock seems to have been here from the time of Prince Toshihito, but not to have been as high then as it is now. The teahouse itself is said to have been brought from the Imadegawa residence of the Hachijō family, where it had been

situated next to a well. Historical sources suggest that it was transferred here by Prince Noritada around 1647.

The building is of a very simple type, inspired by tiny commercial teahouses serving travelers along mountainous roads. The posts are unbarked logs, and the floor plan consists of only four tatami mats placed in a U-shaped pattern around an unfloored space where the hearth is situated (*Figure 14*). In Prince Noritada's day, the atmosphere of a mountain rest house was accentuated by hanging a typical shop-curtain (*noren*) along the front of the building. This consisted of alternating strips of dark blue and white cloth, joined only at the top. In the spring, this Japanese equivalent of a shop sign carried a legend saying "Yoshino Teashop," after the name of a location famous for its cherry blossoms, and in the autumn it was changed to one reading "Tatsuta Teashop," after the name of a place famous for its colorful maple trees. This practice is preserved today. The name Shōka-tei means roughly "Flower-Appreciation Pavilion" and was chosen because this part of the garden has quite a few cherry trees.

Just beyond the Shōka-tei, the garden path divides into two lanes, thus providing an exception to the general rule about tour gardens. The path on the right leads across an earth-covered bridge to the front lawn of the main house, and the one on the left extends alongside the pond to the Onrin-dō, whose architectural style is inconsistent with the other Katsura structures. The Onrin-dō is a small ancestral shrine, where cenotaphs of the past heads of the house of Hachijō were kept. On the face of it, the inclusion of a Buddhist-style building in a garden designed for pleasure and amusement seems odd, but it was not unusual in Prince Noritada's time. Similar buildings were constructed in the gardens of both Nagoya Castle and Edo Castle.

From the Onrin-dō, there is an earth-covered bridge leading to an open strip called the Plum Riding Lane. About halfway down the

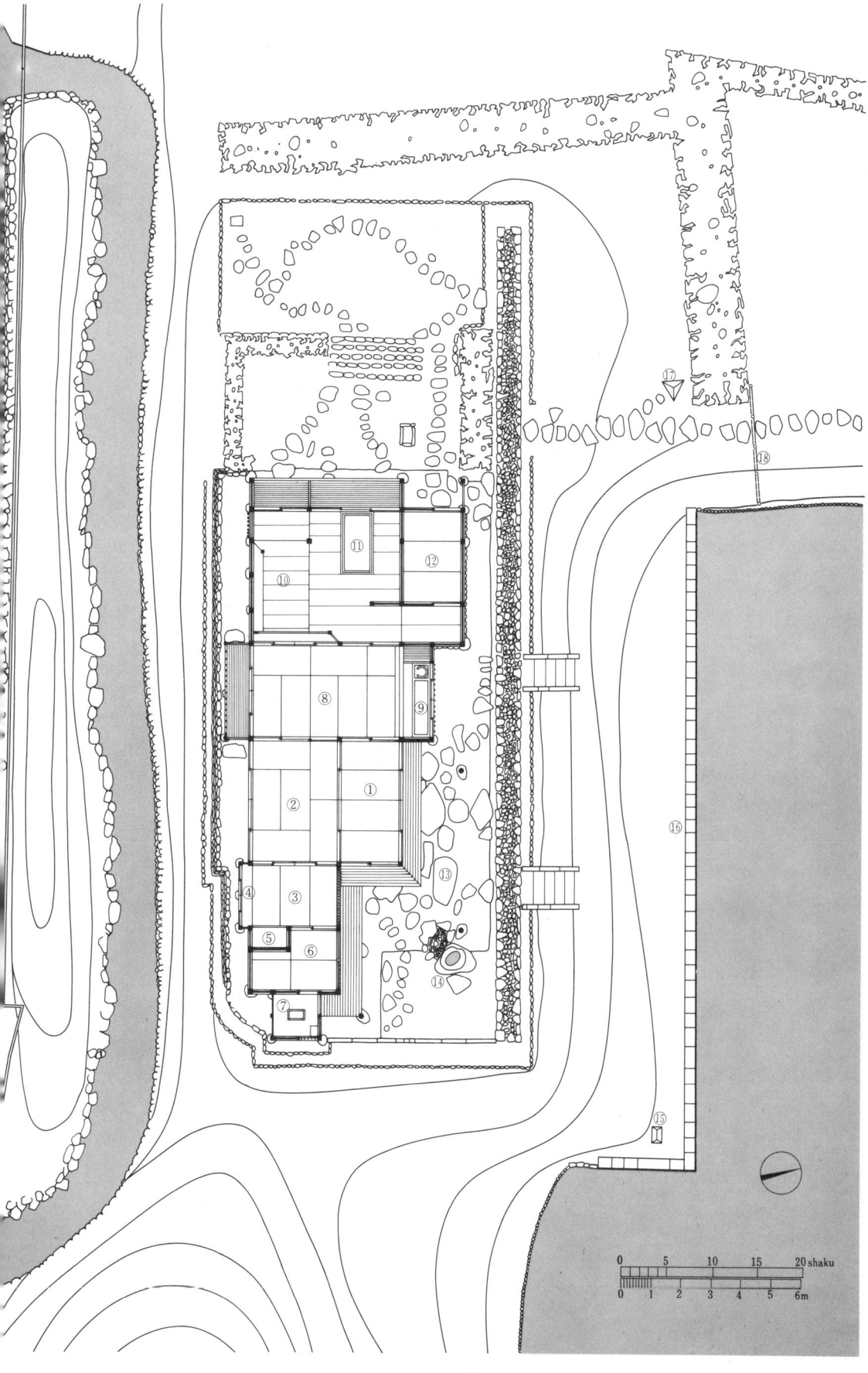

length of this, the path turns toward the left, where the Shōi-ken is situated. This teahouse is in an area apart from the rest of the garden, and in the past there was a small gate midway down the row of stepping stones leading to the building.

That this teahouse is different in character from the others is suggested by its very name. Shōi-ken means "Laughing-Thoughts Pavilion" and is the only name of a building at Katsura that has an abstract meaning. "Moon-Wave," "Pine-Lute," and so on are concrete terms, which, though in some cases inspired by Chinese poetry, connote nothing more than the simple Japanese love of viewing nature in the four seasons. "Laughing-Thoughts," however, is a reference to the decision of the T'ang poet Li Po (701—762) to retire to a hermitage and spend his time laughing at the vanity of the ordinary world. Perhaps for this reason, there is something deliberately foreign about the design of the Shōi-ken (*Figure 15*). In the upper wall of the Entry Room facing the unfloored loggia, for example, there is a very un-Japanese row of six round windows, which give the approaching visitor the somewhat sinister feeling that the building (or is it Li Po?) is laughing at him. In the six-mat Middle Room beyond, the strip of wall beneath the windows is adorned with checkered velvet—a distinctly exotic cloth in seventeenth-century Japan—applied in an eccentric diagonal pattern. The name Shōi-ken itself has alien connotations, for *ken* is a word commonly used to denote buildings in non-Japanese styles.

It is not the visual appearance alone that sets the Shōi-ken apart from the other buildings in the Katsura Palace. The arrangement of the rooms—from the narrow toilet at the southeast end through a series of wider and wider rooms to the kitchen and servants' quarters—suggests that the building was used as an independent house. Prince Noritada may well have built it with the intention of retiring to it from time to

15. Plan of the Shōi-ken and surroundings (mid Edo period).

1. Entry Room	7. Lavatory	13. Unfloored loggia
2. Middle Room (Second Room)	8. Third Room	14. Water basin
3. First Room	9. Pantry in the Third Room	15. Three Lights Lantern
4. *Shoin* window	10. Kitchen	16. Boat mooring
5. Tokonoma in the First Room	11. Hearth	17. Triangular Lantern
6. Storeroom	12. Servants' quarters	18. Site of former gate

time for fairly lengthy periods. It may indeed have been his study, for there is a small room with a *shoin* window overlooking the farmlands outside the palace grounds and thus connecting the building psychologically with the real world rather than the paradisiac garden of pleasure. Whereas the other teahouses are clearly designed for not more than a day's entertainment, the Shōi-ken could serve as a very private residence, and it probably did.

Because of the unusual character of this building, many have theorized that it is the latest of the structures in the palace. According to the most widely accepted version of the *Record of the Country House at Katsura*, however, the landscape paintings on the door panels were executed by Kanō Naonobu, who went to Edo in 1647 and is not known ever to have returned to Kyoto. It consequently seems likely that the paintings, along with the building itself, were completed in 1647 or thereabouts.

As mentioned earlier, the Chikurin-tei, or "Bamboo-Grove Pavilion," no longer exists today. According to a late version of the *Record of the Country House at Katsura*, the "little teahouse in the melon patch" itself was the Chikurin-tei, but this statement seems to be an emendation to the document and does not appear in more reliable versions. In the Ikeda family's "Scenes Inside and Outside the Capital," there is a thatched-roof cabin in a bamboo grove on the edge of the Katsura River which may very well have been the pavilion in question (*see Figure 6, 95*). The hut in the picture seems to have been of the simplest possible construction, and one would suppose that a building of this type, situated where it was, might well be washed away during one of the Katsura River's fairly frequent floods. It could quite possibly have been destroyed and rebuilt any number of times. The latest record testifying to its existence dates from 1765, and one may suppose that it disappeared for good not long after that.

The New Palace

Tokugawa Iemitsu died on May 29, 1651, and was succeeded as shogun by the ten-year-old Tokugawa Ietsuna. By this time, the domestic and foreign policies of the shogunate were so firmly established that the succession of a mere boy to the office of shogun posed no danger to Tokugawa rule. At the same time, actual government passed into the hands of a committee of high officials under the leadership of Hoshina Masayuki, a younger brother of Iemitsu who had been adopted into a different family. One result of this shift in power was that the shogunate ceased to embark on venturesome new policies such as had been carried out during the reigns of the first three shoguns. By and large, the tendency henceforward was for the officials in charge to try to maintain the status quo in all matters. As a natural consequence, extravagant visits by the shogun to Kyoto and by courtiers to Edo came to an end. On June 23, 1651, less than a month after Iemitsu's death, the ex-Emperor Go-Mizunoo became a Buddhist priest, much to the annoyance of the shogunate's Confucianist advisers. Three years later, one of Go-Mizunoo's many sons,* Prince Sachi, became the adopted heir of Prince Noritada.

Although the house of Hachijō was a collateral line of the imperial clan, until now it had had relatively close connections with the warrior class. As we have seen, Prince Toshihito's wife, who incidentally was now known as Jōshō-in, had come from the Kyōgoku family, and Prince Noritada's consort from the Maeda family. Prince Noritada's younger brother even became an adopted son in the Owari branch of the Tokugawa family. All in all, the Hachijō were on more friendly

---

* Go-Mizunoo is said to have had thirty-two children, of whom fifteen were boys. He was succeeded by a daughter because the sons born before his abdication had died. Three sons born later eventually became emperors.

terms with the shogunate than any of the other imperial families (that is, the principal and the other collateral lines). Such being the case, Prince Noritada must have thought long and hard before adopting the son of the ex-emperor, who had time and again displayed his resentment against the shogunate. If the Tokugawa government objected to the adoption, however, it did not do so openly, and a year later Prince Sachi became Prince Yasuhito, third head of the house of Hachijō.

When Prince Noritada acquired a son, it became necessary by imperial tradition to build a separate house for him. This was done at the compound in Imadegawa, and it may well have been done at Katsura too. This would explain the New Palace (Shin-Goten), a large annex that now forms the southernmost wing of the main house. If this theory is correct, it may be assumed that the construction work was carried out shortly after the prince's adoption in 1654.

On the other hand, since the New Palace is also called the "Imperial-Visit Palace" (Miyuki Goten), it has been maintained by some scholars that the annex was built to accommodate the ex-Emperor Go-Mizunoo on one of his visits to Katsura. The ex-emperor is known to have gone to the palace on three occasions, once in 1658 and twice in 1663. The first visit was an unofficial one, no doubt because the shogunate would have frowned upon a ceremonial display of friendship between the truculent ex-emperor and the complaisant Prince Noritada. It seems unlikely that any extraordinary preparations were undertaken at the palace at this time. The other two visits, however, were made after 1662 (Prince Noritada died on August 20 of that year), and the shogunate could hardly object to the ex-emperor's being royally received by Prince Yasuhito, who was his own son. There is every indication that the prince entertained his revered father as lavishly as his means permitted. Go-Mizunoo, for his part, treated his later two journeys as formal imperial progresses, taking along with him a large retinue that included concubines, imperial princes and princesses, and a number of courtiers. He was welcomed with great ceremony in the New Palace (i.e., the Imperial-Visit Palace), and thanks to this event, it is certain that the New Palace was built before the end of 1663. In short, this addition to the house must have been made during the ten years between 1654 and 1663.

In architectural style, the New Palace closely resembles the Manju-in in Kyoto, a residence built in 1656 by Prince Noritada's younger brother, the Priestly Imperial Prince Ryōshō. In particular, the famous Katsura shelving in the Imperial Dais of the New Palace, and to an even greater degree the shelving in the Dressing Room, are variations on the style seen at the Manju-in (Figure 16). The railings on the verandas and ornamental door fittings are also comparable in style. The comparison suggests that the New Palace and the Manju-in were constructed around the same time. This supposition is strengthened by the fact that the paintings on the door panels of the cabinets in the Dressing Room bear the seal of Kanō Tan'yū, who, during the decade when the New Palace must have been built, visited Kyoto only in 1655. It can be no great mistake, therefore, to conclude that the New Palace was indeed built in 1655 or 1656, as indicated by stylistic considerations.

Nevertheless, it should be noted that the Imperial Dais in the First Room of the New Palace, which is one of the most important features of the whole annex, shows signs of having been rebuilt. Most likely, an earlier and simpler arrangement was replaced by a more imposing one in 1663 in deference to the ex-Emperor Go-Mizunoo. In sum, then, the New Palace was built in 1655 or 1656 for the use of Prince Yasuhito and remodeled in 1663 on the occasion of Go-Mizunoo's visit.

A question remains as to who paid for the New Palace. Since it was built simultaneously with the construction of a new house in Kyoto at

16. The Twilight Room, built in 1656 at the Manju-in, Kyoto, is a late example of *shoin* architecture, which shows the influence of the *sukiya* style.

the Imadegawa site, it is most unlikely that Prince Noritada could have financed both projects alone. Furthermore, because of the new connection between the Hachijō and the ex-emperor, it is virtually certain that the shogunate would have refused to assist. The most likely supposition is that costs were defrayed, at least in part, by Prince Noritada's wealthy father-in-law, Lord Maeda of Kaga. Local historical materials preserved in Ishikawa Prefecture (formerly Kaga) tend to confirm this theory.

Prince Yakahito and Bruno Taut

In 1665, two years after Go-Mizunoo's third visit to Katsura, Prince Yasuhito died prematurely at the age of twenty-three. With this unfortunate event, the glory in which the Katsura Palace had been bathed for the previous twenty years became a thing of the past.

With the death of Prince Yasuhito, the house of Hachijō entered a period of misfortune. Perhaps the saddest event, as far as the Katsura Palace is concerned, was the death in 1669 of Jōshō-in, who had married Prince Toshihito in 1616 and had known the palace throughout its existence to date. She was one of a handful of people who were familiar with both the earlier and the later versions of the palace. After the death of the ex-Emperor Go-Mizunoo in 1680, there remained no one who had any direct knowledge of the palace as it had been in its prime.

The fourth head of the Hachijō family was Prince Osahito, the eldest son of the Emperor Go-Sai. He died in 1675 at the age of twenty, and his successor, Prince Hisahito, the ninth son of Go-Sai, died in 1689 at the age of eighteen. When Prince Saku, the eighth son of the Emperor Reigen, succeeded as the sixth heir, the name of the family was changed to Tokiwai in the hope of averting further misfortune. This tactic proved ineffective, however, for Prince Saku died in 1692 when only three years old, and the name Tokiwai was immediately deleted from the official records. The Katsura Palace thus had four owners in thirty years, all of whom died at an early age. In these circumstances, it is hardly surprising that no important changes were made in the buildings or garden during this period. The palace, however, had acquired considerable fame during its earlier years, and, as can be seen from the "Complete Drawing of Prince Katsura's Country House" (*Katsura-no-miya Gobessō Zenzu*), which dates from 1697, it was still in a relatively well-preserved state at that time (*Figure 17*).

After the death of Prince Saku, no one was appointed head of the house of Hachijō for four years, doubtless because of the series of untimely deaths the family had suffered. In 1696, when the Emperor Reigen made another of his sons heir to the Hachijō estate, he renamed the family Kyōgoku. The new head was named Imperial Prince Ayahito in the following year. Since he was regarded as the first Prince Kyōgoku, the name Hachijō was henceforward a matter only of historical record. It was around this time that various legends concerning the early history of the Katsura Palace began to take form.

After the second change of name, all went reasonably well for a time. An heir was born to Prince Ayahito in 1704, and in 1709 this son was named Imperial Prince Yakahito, the second head of the house of Kyōgoku. This prince, who lived to be sixty-five, resembled Prince Toshihito and Prince Noritada in that he had a taste for poetry and the culture associated with the imperial tradition. He took a great interest in the Katsura Palace and searched among the documents preserved in his household for historical sources relating to its origin. By this time, however, the story of the palace's beginnings had disappeared behind the veil of history; no detailed or reliable materials were available to the prince. It happened that Prince Yakahito was a great admirer of gardens designed by Kobori Enshū (1579–1647). Though a daimyo, Enshū was known far and wide for his cultural attainments. He studied the art of tea under Furuta Oribe, himself a favored disciple of Sen no Rikyū, and was so highly reputed as a tea-master that he was engaged to give lessons to Tokugawa Iemitsu. In addition, Enshū practiced Zen at the Daitoku-ji and studied Japanese poetry under Reizen Tamemitsu, one of the leading orthodox poets of the age. His instructor in

17. The "Complete Drawing of Prince Katsura's Country House," c. 1688–1704. National Diet Library.

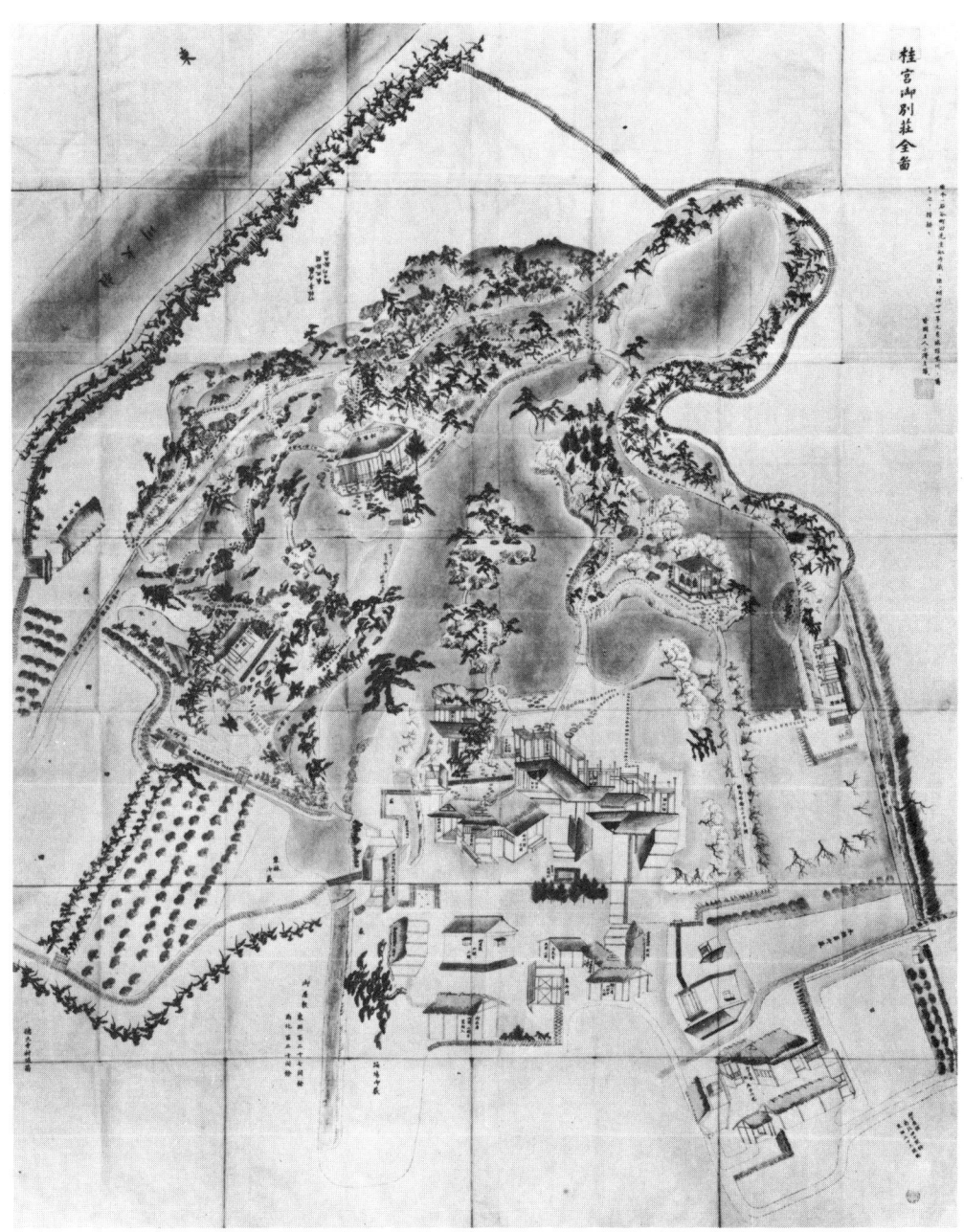

calligraphy was Shōkadō Shōjō, who is counted among the three great masters of this art in the early Edo period. Like all tea-masters, Enshū was deeply interested in ceramics; he is credited with having been the guiding spirit for a number of well-known kilns in the province of which he was governor. It is hardly surprising that he also developed a new concept of environmental design as applied to architecture and gardens.

Possibly because of his fondness for Enshū's work, Prince Yakahito arrived at the conclusion that the Katsura Palace, or at least its garden, must have been designed by him. This was probably no more than a theory. The palace and garden were built over a fairly long period of time, and it is unlikely that they were the work of one man, even if Kobori Enshū's concept was dominant. Furthermore, there is a distinct possibility that Yakahito had a private reason for crediting Enshū with the whole design, for he is known to have borrowed money from the Kobori family, Enshū's progeny.

Nevertheless, after Prince Yakahito's death in 1767, the Enshū legend took root, and by the end of the eighteenth century it was widely accepted as fact. Indeed, a book on famous gardens in Kyoto, published in 1799, states not only that Enshū oversaw the construction of Katsura Palace, but also that he did so on the order of Toyotomi Hideyoshi. As noted earlier, the house of Hachijō did not even come into possession of the land in Katsura village until after Hideyoshi's death. Prince Yoshihito's country house could not, therefore, have been built until later. But legends have no value unless they are interesting, nor is it by any means unusual to embroider them in such a way as to create a link with a very famous man. The curious feature of stories like this is that they nearly always have some basis in fact, no matter how badly distorted. The idea that Hideyoshi ordered the building of the Katsura Palace is no doubt founded on the dim recollection that the

Hachijō line had been established at Hideyoshi's behest. Until the end of the Tokugawa period in 1868, the Katsura legend continued to grow and spawn new legends and stories, for there was no one around who knew the truth.

At the time of the fall of the shogunate, the palace was in a dilapidated condition. People alive at the time of the Meiji Restoration have said that during the years immediately following it, the palace was vandalized by samurai traveling back and forth on the San'indō Highway. According to one account, the intruders ruined quite a few of the twenty-four stone lanterns in the garden by using parts of them as weights for contests and displays of physical prowess.

Prince Yakahito was succeeded by Prince Kinhito, who was followed by Prince Takehito, a son of the Emperor Kōkaku; but in 1810 the name of the family was again changed—from Kyōgoku to Katsura. Prince Takehito is considered the first head of the Katsura line. He was succeeded by Prince Misahito, a son of the Emperor Ninkō, and then by the Imperial Princess Sumiko, Prince Misahito's elder sister. With the death of the princess in 1881, the Hachijō-Kyōgoku-Katsura line passed quietly out of existence, and the Katsura establishment became a detached imperial palace under the jurisdiction of the Imperial Household Ministry (now Agency).

During the Meiji period (1868–1912), very few people were familiar with the palace, and those who knew it accepted the legends that had grown up in the eighteenth century or afterward. There was no scholarly research into its past, though the government took steps to repair the buildings and the gardens. In 1927, Eisaku Toyama published a study in which he exposed and refuted the Kobori Enshū myth, but this was read only by a limited number of scholars. Most people continued to believe the legend.

Then in May, 1933, the German architect Bruno Taut (1880–1938)

took refuge in Japan from the Nazis. Describing himself as a "vagabond artist," he spent the next three years familiarizing himself with the manners and customs of Japan, and particularly with historical Japanese architecture. He visited the Ise Shrine (*Figure 18*), the old Imperial Palace in Kyoto (*Figure 19*), the Shugaku-in Detached Palace just northeast of Kyoto, the Tōshō-gū in Nikko, the Katsura Detached Palace, and a number of old farmhouses (*Figure 20*). He then published several critiques that both startled and delighted the Japanese intellectuals of the time.

Taut earnestly advised that the Japanese people, who since the Meiji period had concerned themselves all too single-mindedly with the

19. The residential quarters of the Imperial Palace, Kyoto.

18. The shrine buildings at Ise are of particular interest for they preserve a form of residential architecture from the pre-Buddhist period.

adoption of Western ways, should rediscover their own traditional arts. Setting up an antithesis between the emperor and the shogun, he argued that the Katsura Palace, which represented the imperial tradition, was architecture of eternal and universal value, like the Parthenon, whereas the shogun's mausoleum at Nikko represented sheer architectural decadence.

Yet even Bruno Taut thought that the Katsura Palace had been designed by the daimyo and tea-master Kobori Enshū. Taut also accepted the groundless legend that in giving the commission to design and construct the palace to Enshū, the owner, Prince Toshihito, had

20. Farmhouses, Shirakawa Village, Gifu Prefecture.

told him (1) not to worry about the cost, (2) not to worry about the completion date, and (3) not to show it to him until it was done. No doubt these apocryphal conditions seemed highly enviable from the viewpoint of a modern German architect.

Obviously it would be a mistake from the historical standpoint to take Bruno Taut's theories concerning the Katsura Palace too seriously. But it is nevertheless true that owing to his efforts, the palace came to be known throughout the world as an outstanding example of traditional Japanese architecture.

THE AESTHETICS OF KATSURA: MANNERISM

The Social Background

In an entry for the fourth month of 1603, only two months after the appointment of Tokugawa Ieyasu as shogun, a source entitled *Records of This Reign* (*Tōdai-ki*) mentions that "something called the kabuki dance" had been introduced in Kyoto by a woman named Okuni and was enjoying a great vogue among high and low alike. This is the first historical reference to the Okuni kabuki, which was the precursor of the Kabuki drama (*Figure 21*). The same source goes on to say that Okuni had previously been a shrine maiden at the Izumo Shrine, and that her forte was dressing up like a two-sworded samurai and dallying with teahouse girls on the stage. She is further said to have danced frequently at Fushimi Castle and to have inspired many imitators in other parts of the country, but to have been unwelcome to Tokugawa Hidetada, who became the second shogun.

The shogun's new capital at Edo was at this time bustling with construction work and enjoying the prosperity that comes from rapid expansion, but Kyoto, caught as it was between Edo and the Toyotomi stronghold in Osaka, was going through a period of tense anxiety. Everyone recognized that the city might soon be ravaged once again by war, for the possibility of open conflict between the Tokugawa and the Toyotomi was all too evident.

On the surface it appeared that the authority of the Tokugawa had been firmly established, but by the standards of many, Ieyasu remained a vassal of the house of Toyotomi and was thus obligated eventually to

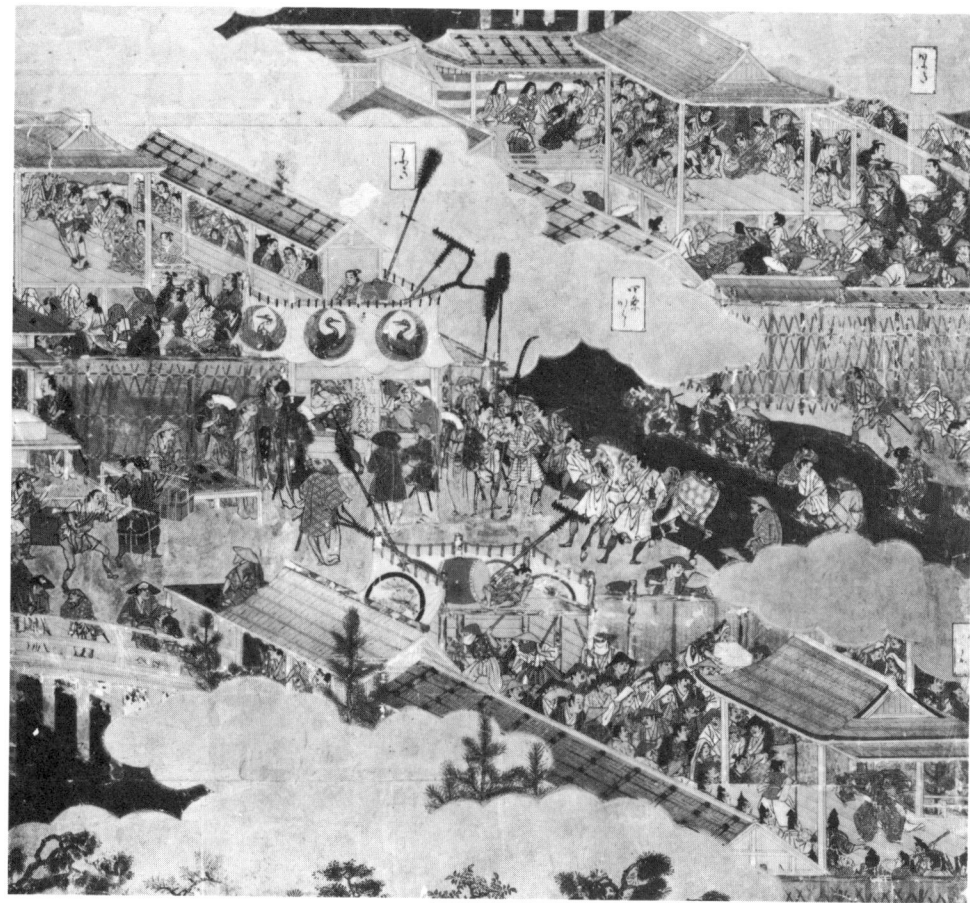

21. The kabuki dance being performed in three theaters on Shijō Avenue next to the Kamo River. From a pair of six-panel screens entitled "Scenes Inside and Outside the Capital," early seventeenth century. Formerly owned by the Funaki family, now in the Tokyo National Museum.

hand over the reins of government to Hideyori. Even Ieyasu himself proceeded with caution in asserting his primacy over Hideyoshi's heir. Indeed, in some respects, he actually fostered the impression that he was merely a caretaker for the young Hideyori. In 1603, for example, he ordered the feudal lords to pay their New Year's respects at Osaka

Castle on the first day of the year and to visit him on the second day. In the same year, he honored a pledge to Hideyoshi by having his seven-year-old granddaughter, Lady Sen, betrothed to Hideyori. When he was himself appointed shogun, he had Hideyori made minister of internal affairs—a step regarded by many as a prelude to having the young man promoted to the office of grand chancellor, which had been held by his father. On the seventh anniversary of Hideyoshi's death, Ieyasu sponsored a great memorial service and festival in Kyoto as a means of showing his devotion to his deceased master.

All of this, however, was part of a plan to mollify the numerous supporters of the Toyotomi in the Kyoto-Osaka region, and few observers regarded Ieyasu's efforts to preserve peace as anything more than temporary. It was generally believed that war would come sooner or later.

Such being the case, much of the populace of Kyoto and Osaka was inclined to forget about tomorrow and live for the pleasures of the moment. It was in this atmosphere that the Okuni kabuki dances and other frivolous amusements flourished in the capital.

The word "kabuki" is a form of *katamuku*, which means to be slanted away from the vertical, or, in other words, to be eccentric. It was applied to things that went against the grain of ordinary common sense or morals, such as the spectacle of a transvestite woman cavorting on a stage with waitresses and the like. The overtones of sexual perversion titillated the audiences, and the stories enacted by the players transported them into a strange world of pleasures far removed from the realities of the times. A spirit of immorality was in the air, and the imperial court was not immune. In 1609, it was discovered that two of the Emperor Go-Yōzei's concubines, Hirohashi and Karahashi, had been carrying on illicit affairs with a number of high noblemen, including the well-known poet and calligrapher Karasumaru Mitsuhiro.

Infuriated, the emperor wanted to have all persons involved executed, but Ieyasu reduced their punishment to banishment. Go-Yōzei gave notice of his wish to abdicate, and though he was persuaded to postpone this step for a time, in 1611 he ceded the throne to Go-Mizunoo.

It was ostensibly because of immorality at the court that the shogunate issued the five-article Rules for the Nobility of 1613. One regulation actually stated that noblemen were not to wander about in the streets of the city either in the daytime or at night, unless they were on official business. The real purpose of the document, however, was political, and the key article was the first, which stated that noblemen were to devote their time to the pursuit of scholarship. The Rules for the Nobility were remarkable not so much for their content as for their having been issued at all. Since the ancient past, laws and regulations had in general been enacted in the name of the emperor. True, he had long been controlled by the military leaders, but until now, codes of conduct enacted by the military government had applied only to the warrior class. The shogunate's Rules for the Nobility represent an assertion of direct authority over the court, and the first article was a clear warning that the courtiers must confine themselves to activities other than politics.

In 1615, shortly after the battle of Osaka, the Tokugawa government issued the seventeen-article Rules for the Imperial Court and the Nobility, which were even more explicit and high-handed than the code of 1613. Whereas the earlier regulations had applied only by implication to the emperor, the new regulations stated specifically that the sovereign's primary duty was scholarship. Other articles spelled out what the emperor could and could not do with his time. This was the first occasion on which a military ruler had ever issued direct orders concerning the emperor's conduct.

22. A festival procession passing Nijō Castle. From a pair of six-panel screens entitled "Scenes Inside and Outside the Capital," 1615–18. Formerly owned by the Ikeda family, now in the Museum of Fine Arts, Okayama.

Since ancient times the emperor and the court had considered it their duty to encourage scholarship and the arts. This, however, had been only a secondary function arising from their exalted position and their long cultural tradition. Their primary function was, and had always been, at least in theory, to govern the country, and it was a distinct departure from tradition for the Tokugawa shogunate to state otherwise. At the same time, the order limiting the emperor to scholarly pursuits may be regarded as no more than a recognition of the facts of life, for it is true that under the Tokugawa government the emperor had no political authority. Furthermore, both he and his courtiers were subject to supervision and control by the shogunate's magistrate in Nijō Castle (*Figure 22*).

The Aesthetics of Alienation

The Tokugawa government was not content merely to confine the activities of the nobility to the realms of art and scholarship. It even segregated their living quarters from the rest of the people. A wall was built around "Nobility Town" (*Figure 23*), and movements of the courtiers into and out of this district were strictly supervised. Not even the emperor or the ex-emperor was exempt. Shortly after the death of Tokugawa Iemitsu in June, 1651, for example, the ex-Emperor Go-Mizunoo attempted to make a trip to Shirakawa, east of the capital, but was denied permission. It was this incident that led him to take the tonsure and become a Buddhist priest.

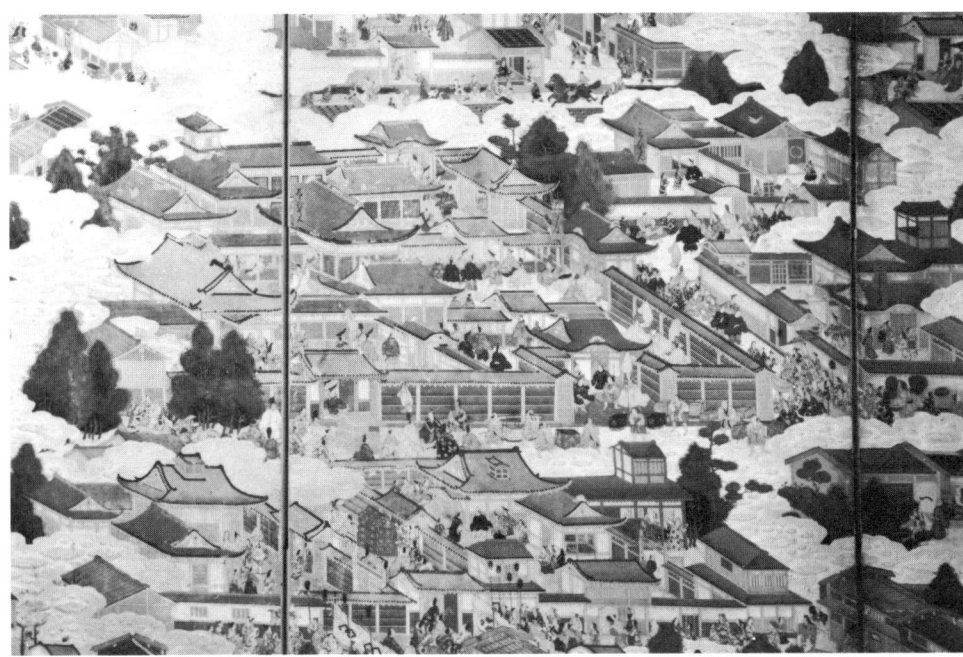

23. "Nobility Town." From a pair of six-panel screens entitled "Scenes Inside and Outside the Capital," 1615–18. Formerly owned by the Ikeda family, now in the Museum of Fine Arts, Okayama.

The relocation of the palace and the houses of the nobility to the northeast section of Kyoto was completed in 1613, the year in which the five-article Rules for the Nobility were instituted. By this time, the first reconstruction of the Imperial Palace undertaken by the shogunate was finished. Built as nearly as possible in the style of the Heian period, the palace included all the buildings where great affairs of state had once taken place, as well as private quarters for the emperor and his many consorts. Over and above this, the shogunate added to the plan a separate hall of study (*gakumon-jo*), which served to emphasize the role that the Tokugawa government expected the sovereign to play.

One of the men charged by the shogunate with constructing the various buildings in the new palace was Kobori Enshū, the man legendarily regarded as the designer of Katsura Palace. Enshū's style as applied to architecture and gardens was a synthesis of the elegance and grace of the imperial court tradition with the austere rusticity favored by Sen no Rikyū. This combination is by no means as farfetched as it sounds, because Rikyū's *sabi*—an aesthetic ideal connoting seclusion, quietude, pastoral simplicity, and closeness to nature—was akin to a certain escapist element that had long been a prominent feature of traditional Japanese culture. By simply toning down some of the more severe features of *sabi*, Enshū was able to fuse the general concept with the more colorful, elegant, and sentimental canons of taste associated with the Heian court. The result, which has been aptly described as "beautiful *sabi*," received the wholehearted approval of the emperor and the nobility of Enshū's day, whose financial circumstances were not such that they could have duplicated the lavishness of the Heian court to begin with. "Beautiful *sabi*" furnished these alienated aristocrats with the illusion that they were enjoying the elegance and richness of Heian times. The more isolated they became from the society around them, the more highly they treasured this dream.

Even in the Heian period, the idea of retiring to a secluded mountain hut, remote from the cares of this world, appealed strongly to the creators of aristocratic culture. This attraction was no doubt based to a large extent on the love of nature that tends to be inspired by Japan's scenic beauty and seasonal variety. In a country so liberally endowed with botanical riches and magnificent landscapes, not to speak of a temperate, though constantly changing, climate, it would be strange indeed if sensitivity to nature and a longing to be immersed in it were not an intrinsic part of the national psychology. In the Heian period in particular, nature was idealized as the antithesis of worldly vanity, and the mountain hut nestling in peaceful natural surroundings became a symbol of escape from the harshness of reality. No doubt this glorification of nature was based to some degree on the idea of the Taoist immortal and the quietistic philosophy of Lao-tzu, as well as on the ancient Confucian dictum that "the wise man loves the streams, the benevolent man loves the mountains." The Buddhist ideal of renouncing the world in order to find truth must also have exercised an important influence. At the same time, a yearning to live close to nature would have been a prominent element in the Japanese psyche even without external stimuli.

What must not be forgotten in this connection is that although to judge from the poetry and novels of the time, Heian aristocrats talked continually of their weariness with this world of sorrows, most of them spent their time angling for official ranks or pursuing their various love affairs. They liked the *idea* of the simple hut in the mountains, but they were usually willing to settle for something that suggested it in their town houses in Kyoto. In the *Tale of Genji*, for example, a passage describing the garden of an urban dwelling says, "It was poignantly lonely and desolate—only the snow settled warmly on the pine trees, but one felt the plaintive beauty of a village in the mountains." The feeling of the mountain hut was a desideratum for residential environments in general. In actuality, the Heian noblemen lived in large, rambling mansions, and their efforts to achieve the mountain-hut effect were expended largely on their gardens. It is no accident that the oldest Japanese book on gardening techniques, a late eleventh-century work entitled *On Constructing Gardens* (*Sakutei-ki*), emphasizes the importance of reproducing natural mountain settings.

The mountain hut of Heian times was to a large extent a myth. Even the wealthiest of the aristocrats, despite their concern for atmosphere and taste, did not go out in the distant mountains and build hovels for themselves. At the most, they constructed country houses in places like Omuro, Saga, Katsura, Ōhara, and Uji, all of which were on the Yamashiro Plain surrounding Kyoto. The original inspiration, therefore, may have been the same as that which led Chinese philosophers and Buddhist hermits to retire to mountain retreats, but the result was very different.

During the medieval period, the importation from China of Zen Buddhism and the culture associated with it gave new life to the mountain-hut idea, this time in the form of a tea cult in which solitude and bucolic settings were ideals. A degree of concreteness was achieved by tea-masters who designed teahouses and tearooms after the fashion of simple rural buildings. The name *sukiya*, which implies rusticity, informality, and a degree of whimsy, was applied to the teahouse style, both the development and the popularization of which owed much to the efforts of Sen no Rikyū. It should not be overlooked, however, that Rikyū was concerned, not with nature in the raw, but with certain natural settings that might be reproduced artificially in an urban residence. The following statement is attributed to him: "A mountain hut is a house as rustic and unpretentious as a reed-covered shanty on a beach. It is an unadorned dwelling in a lonely setting, where the cherry

blossoms and maple leaves of last year have all been buried under the snow." This has nothing to do with nature as such: it is the description of a pseudonatural effect that can be achieved by artifice. By adding to Rikyū's conceptualized version of the mountain hut certain elements of delicacy and gracefulness from the Heian tradition, Kobori Enshū created "beautiful *sabi*."

Enshū's style dominated the early Edo period, which is to say the years from about 1615 to 1650 or so. It was employed in the rebuilding of the Imperial Palace as well as in the houses of high noblemen, and its influence was even felt at Edo Castle, the stronghold of the Tokugawa shoguns. Prince Toshihito, a cultural arbiter at the court and a man who but for an accident might have been emperor, naturally followed the Enshū fashion in building his house at Katsura.

As we have seen, by the middle of the eighteenth century, the entire design of the palace and garden was attributed to Enshū. Much research has failed to yield documentary evidence proving that he was connected with the palace in its earlier stages, but there is good reason to believe that he played an important part at the time of Prince Noritada's reconstruction.

It happens that Enshū's father, Shinsuke, was also an expert architect and garden designer. Serving as a construction official under Hideyoshi, he took part in the planning and building of both the Hall of the Great Buddha at the Hōkō-ji in Kyoto and the castle at Fushimi, where Hideyoshi retired in his old age. It was no doubt the great skill and talent displayed by Shinsuke and Enshū in the field of environmental design that led to their being patronized by the Tokugawa shogunate after Hideyoshi's death. In their ability to survive the shift from Hideyoshi to Ieyasu, they had something in common with Prince Toshihito. Certainly it would have been difficult to find among the daimyo serving as officials under the Tokugawa a man better equipped than Kobori Enshū to understand and sympathize with the nobility whom the shogunate had banished to the world of scholarship and the arts.

It was not by chance, then, that the design of the Katsura Palace is in the style of Enshū, in its psychological and philosophical implications, as well as in its visible aspects. The dream that came to Prince Toshihito as he was tossed about in the agitated political currents of his time was given its perfect expression in Enshū's "beautiful *sabi*," which embodied both the illusion of the mountain hut and the elegance of Heian court life.

In this sense, the Katsura Palace may be said to represent the aesthetics of alienation or of escapism. It is therefore fundamentally different in character from other famous works of Japanese architecture, such as the great shrine to the sun goddess at Ise and the Tōshō-gū in Nikko, which were built to satisfy a realistic social or political need.

A Stylistic Paradox: Eclectic Classicism

Prince Toshihito was well versed in classic Japanese literature. He studied Japanese poetry under Hosokawa Yūsai and at the age of only twenty-four received a diploma from his teacher certifying that he had mastered the secrets of the *Anthology of Ancient and Modern Poetry* (*Kokin Wakashū*), compiled in the Heian period by imperial command and considered alongside the *Man'yōshū* as one of the greatest collections of Japanese poetry. In addition, he was well acquainted with the *Tale of Genji*, the *Tales of Utsubo*, and other masterpieces of Heian-period prose. He devoted much time to the study of Chinese poetry and philosophy, as was expected of the well-educated Japanese

man, and he practiced many of the traditional Japanese arts and elegances, including calligraphy, painting, flower arrangement, the tea ceremony, the way of incense, music, riding, and court football.* In short, he was the sort of well-rounded man of taste who had always been an ideal in Japanese court circles.

Prince Noritada appears to have been even more deeply immersed in scholarship and the arts than his father. Sano Shōeki, one of the most important cultural figures among the Kyoto bourgeoisie of the time, wrote the following about him in a collection of essays entitled *Nigiwaigusa*, published in 1682:

> In the Kan'ei period [1624–1647], there was a truly noble imperial prince named Noritada, the head of the house of Hachijō. He was so graceful in body and so kind in spirit that one wondered whether indeed he could have been born of human parents. When he was young, he was thin and inclined toward sickness, and because of this his heart was seldom happy and gay.
>
> One day it was suggested to him that he try playing *kemari*, but no one could persuade him to go out on the ball court. Then the people around him urged him to try playing indoors and prepared a room for the purpose. He began playing, and as the days went by, he seemed happier. Finally, he ventured onto the court, and after that he invited Prince Asukai Masaaki and other courtiers to play with him. His body grew healthier, and his spirits became more cheerful. By and by, he decided to build a house on the property he

* *Kemari*, a form of football played at court since the sixth century or earlier. The players gathered in a circle within a square court and kicked a leather ball back and forth, attempting to prevent it from touching the ground. Rather than as a casual game, *kemari* was regarded as an art of sorts.

owned in Katsura, west of the capital, where there had been a teahouse since the time of the former prince [Toshihito]. He himself went many times to the place and engaged workmen to build various pavilions. He also built an artificial hill and made a dam by means of which water was introduced from the Katsura River.

He was fascinated with a passage in the *Tale of Genji* that told about a garden where the color of the flowers, the songs of the birds, and the approach to the middle island were all strange and beautiful—how there were Chinese-style boats rowed by boys in Chinese costume with their hair tied up with bright ribbons behind; how the color of the wisteria was reflected in the water, and mountain-kerria blossoms overflowed from the banks of the pond.* He thereupon directed that the scene be reproduced exactly as described in the novel. People who saw the place said with astonishment that it was just as though the glories of past ages had reappeared in this world.

He invited the famous and fashionable tea-masters of the day and served tea to them in the teahouses. They were invariably astonished to learn that he had designed all this himself. One tea-master said that he had once gone to Miyajima [the Itsukushima Shrine] and concluded that nothing could be more beautiful than the sight there of the sea stretching out to the south, west, and east of the shrine corridors, but that of all the views he had seen here and there, only Katsura and Miyajima were truly the sights of a lifetime.

* The description in question is in Book Three, Chapter Six, of the *Tale of Genji*. Sano has paraphrased the original.

It is of special significance here that Prince Noritada was attempting to reproduce at Katsura the world in which the courtiers of the Heian period had lived, as described in the *Tale of Genji*. When Enshū's ideal of ''beautiful *sabi*'' came into contact with the great store of knowledge that Prince Toshihito and Prince Noritada had of the courtly tradition of ages past, the perfect expression of the illusionary mountain hut came into being.

Accordingly, one cannot avoid the conclusion that the basic tone of the Katsura Palace and its garden was founded on a deep reverence for the traditions of the Heian court. Prince Toshihito and, to an even greater extent, Prince Noritada were similar in character and back-

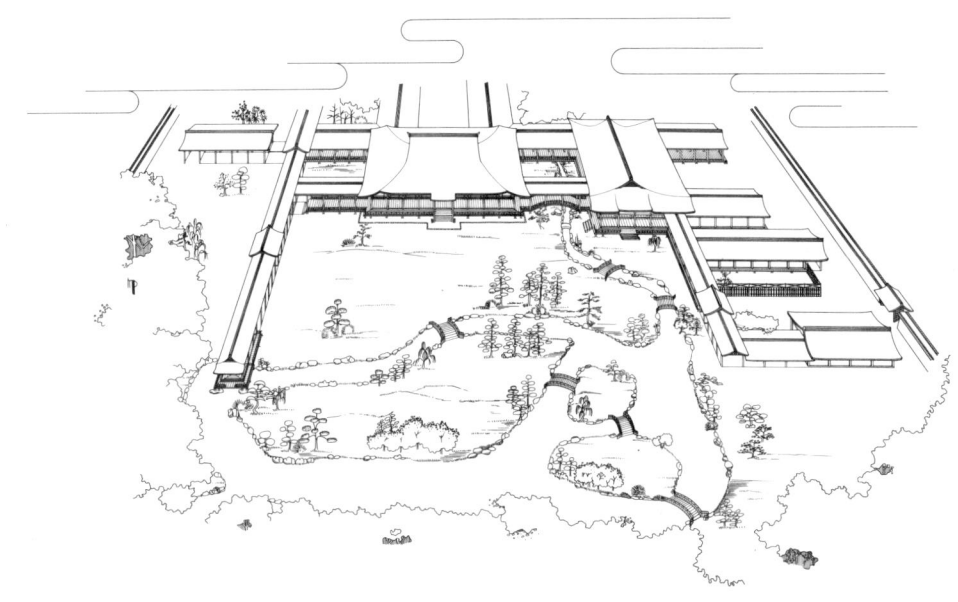

24. Diagram showing a mansion in the *shinden* style.

25. Model of a house in the *shoin* style.

26. A typical example of the *shoin* style is the Guest House, built in 1601, in the Kōjō-in, a subtemple of the Onjō-ji, Otsu.

ground to the Shining Prince in the *Tale of Genji*, and they sought to build at Katsura a little world of their own where the spirit of the ancient court would reign. The farther the design was removed from the realities of their own time, the stronger the classical touch became. If, for example, one regards the Old Shoin as the equivalent of the main hall of a Heian mansion (*Figure 24*), then the area comprising the *shoin*, the pond, and the Middle Islands may be regarded as a design straight out of the *Tale of Genji*. If one then visualizes the bridge with red-lacquered railings that formerly stood before the Shōkin-tei, the effect is almost exaggeratedly antiquarian.

If, on the other hand, one considers not the larger view, but the details, there are surprisingly numerous features that cannot be described as classical. The Old Shoin itself is related to the pond in the same fashion as the main hall in a Heian mansion, but it is by no means built in the Heian style. Though the *shoin* style is descended from the *shinden* style of Heian times, it is very different in appearance and function (*Figures 25 and 26*). As one goes from the Old Shoin through the Middle Shoin to the New Palace, one finds more and more elements of what in the time of the princes Toshihito and Noritada was regarded as modern design. Indeed, the New Palace is not very different from early versions of the *sukiya*-style house. There exists here, then, a stylistic paradox: though the inspiration comes from the *shinden*-style mansion, the actual main house represents the *shoin* style of the middle ages and the *sukiya* style of the early Edo period. We see in this one building the three main styles used up to that time for the homes of the rich.

The paradox does not end here, however, for the design of the Shōkin-tei and the Shōi-ken was derived from Japanese farmhouses, which were completely outside the aristocratic tradition of the Heian court. Taken as a whole, the Katsura Palace is a veritable museum of

124

Japanese residential architecture, containing samples of all the main historical types. It is impossible to suppose that this juxtaposition of styles employed in different ages by different classes of people was accidental, and one must therefore suppose that the conscious aim was to produce a delightful never-never land full of whimsical contradictions. It is for this reason that "eclectic classicism" seems an apt term for the overall design of the Katsura Palace. There is a conscious, intellectual attempt here to sum up the whole of Japanese culture to date, as reflected in architecture.

A Palace of Intellectual Pleasure

An examination of the various details that make up the Katsura Palace and its garden reveals that the total plan is dominated by what Italians call *concettismo*—a concern for that which is conceptual as opposed to that which is real. Seemingly accidental or capricious features are seen, upon reflection, to be literary allusions, philosophical suggestions, or abstract references to some phase of Japanese life.

A striking example is to be seen in the graceful metal fittings used to open and shut the sliding door panels. In the wooden doors separating the rooms of the New Palace from the outside corridor, for example, there is a set of fittings in the form of baskets of flowers. At a glance, these all look fairly much alike, but closer scrutiny shows that there are four types, each containing flowers associated with one of the seasons—cherry blossoms and wisteria for the spring; cotton roses for the summer; chrysanthemums for the fall; and plum blossoms, camellias, and narcissuses for the winter. We have, then, a deliberate reference to the importance attached in Japanese life and literature to seasonal

variations. Other fixtures suggest the strong distinction that has always been drawn in Japan between city life and life in the countryside. The fittings on the door panels between the Middle Shoin and the Music Room, for instance, are in the form of a wide-brimmed hat worn outdoors by court ladies of the Heian period, and those in the Geppa-rō in the shape of a shuttle suggest the weaving women of Kyoto. By way of contrast, the arrow-shaped fittings in the Shōi-ken bring to mind the rough warriors of the provincial areas, while the pine-needle fittings in the Music Room and the paddle-shaped fittings in the Shōi-ken allude to life on the farm or by the sea.

All these motifs are, of course, highly stylized, rather than realistic, for the ugliness that is an inevitable part of pure realism has been removed. The images have been filtered through the delicate sense of taste that permeates the whole of Japanese court tradition. The idealized patterns that result are consequently in perfect harmony with the make-believe atmosphere that dominates this conceptualized "mountain hut."

The same taste for the abstract is evident throughout the garden, but nowhere more strikingly than in the miniature representations of Amanohashidate, across the pond from the Shōkin-tei, and the Ōi River, slightly farther to the north. The Ōi River scene, which may well have been inspired by a passage in the *Tales of Utsubo* eulogizing the beauties of the Ōi River Gorge, is particularly effective because of its clever understatement. The stream is dammed with a few rocks to create a little waterfall, and the pleasant gurgling of the water as it runs over this drop calls attention to the peaceful quiet of the surroundings. The restful feeling of solitude deep within a mountain setting is better conveyed by this one touch than it would be by a more literal attempt to reproduce the actual scene in miniature.

If symbolism of this sort grows too sentimental, it can easily deteriorate into cuteness, even when the subjects are drawn from the classic *Tale of Genji*. That this does not occur at the Katsura Palace is due to the judicious restraint everywhere in evidence. Intellect is always given precedence over emotion, though not to the extent that anything in the Katsura design could be described as pedantic. The only area that is nonlyrical to the point of being expressionless is the Old Shoin, but even in the freer, less formal parts of the palace, there are frequent reminders that the ideal way of life is that of the intellectual, as exemplified by the great poets and thinkers of China. In the Middle Shoin, for example, we find, in the First Room, Kanō Tan'yū's painting of "Li Po Viewing a Waterfall" and, in the Second Room, Kanō Naonobu's portrayal of the Seven Sages. In the Shōi-ken, as we have already seen, the underlying theme is that of Li Po laughing at the vanity of the ordinary world. The six round "laughing windows" may be regarded as an assertion of intellectual superiority with perhaps a trace of cynicism. In less direct ways, the triumph of mind over emotion is illustrated repeatedly in details of the design. In the First and Second Rooms of the New Palace, for instance, the moon, for all its sentimental connotations, is represented not by a lyrical reproduction, but by door fittings patterned on the Chinese character for "moon," suggesting the importance of the written word as opposed to rhapsodic portrayal. The transoms between the same rooms are decorated with a spare and highly linear variation on the swastika, which brings to the Oriental mind Buddhism and Buddhist philosophy (*Figure 27*).

The emphasis on intellectuality at Katsura accords somehow with modern logic, science, and art. The geometrical patterns seen in the famous Katsura shelving of the Imperial Dais in the New Palace, for example, might have been devised by Mondrian in his later years (*Figure 28*). The Katsura Palace seems to appeal to people of our time more than other well-known examples of traditional Japanese architec-

27. The transom between the First Room and Second Room in the New Palace at Katsura is a variation upon the swastika, which is a sign of good fortune in Buddhist iconography.

28. Piet Mondrian, "Composition in Red, Blue, and Yellow," 1930. Mr. and Mrs. Armand Bartos, New York.

ture, such as the Ise Shrine, the Izumo Shrine, the Hōryū-ji, or the Tōshō-gū in Nikko. Perhaps one reason is that we see here the same sort of geometrical abstraction that Mondrian and others discovered three centuries later. Perhaps, too, it was this similarity to a modern trend in art that caused Bruno Taut, a twentieth-century functionalist, to praise the palace as a masterpiece of environmental design.

Since Taut's time nearly everybody has echoed the idea that the Katsura Palace is an example of functional architecture, but a thorough consideration of the design does not support this view. Taut's modern (and foreign) eye saw the lack of conspicuous frills as an absence of ornamentation as such, whereas in fact there is a wealth of non-

29. Tawaraya Sōtatsu, "Tale of Genji" (*Genji Monogatari-zu Byōbu*), after 1630, a pair of six-panel screens, each 162.7 × 342.4 cm., designated National Treasures. Seika-dō Bunko, Tokyo. The left screen is based on the chapter entitled "The Flood Gauge," and the right, on "A Meeting at the Frontier."

functional decoration. Indeed, it is difficult to imagine anything more decorative in essence than the deliberate inclusion of several different historical styles of architecture in the same compound. Taut was misled by the emphasis on intellectuality, which tends to hide the ornamental aspects. What we see here is not functionalism, but merely economy of expression.

The type of ornamentation seen at Katsura can better be understood by comparison with the works of the great decorative painters, Tawaraya Sōtatsu (active in the earlier decades of the seventeenth century) and Ogata Kōrin (1658–1716). Both of these men were members of the Kyoto merchant class; both had entrée into court society and participated in the general revival of classic art that took place in the imperial capital during the early part of the Edo period.

They are credited with developing a new style of decorative painting related in coloring and in subject matter to the classical art of the Heian and Kamakura periods, though larger in scale and bolder in composition. Sōtatsu's most famous works, a pair of paintings based on the *Tale of Genji* and a second pair inspired by court dancing (*Figures 29 and 30*), deserve special attention in this connection, because they were painted around the same time that the Katsura Palace was built. Both works are notable for their taut composition, their rich symbolism, and their lavish color. The elegantly rounded mountains and pine trees in the Genji paintings bring to mind the curving lines of the lawn at Katsura and the celebrated Sumiyoshi Pine on the tip of the peninsula behind the Geppa-rō. Both in Sōtatsu's paintings and in the Katsura garden, there is a deliberate attempt to achieve the classic elegance of

30. Tawaraya Sōtatsu, "Court Dancing" (*Bugaku-zu Byōbu*), date unknown, one of a pair of two-panel screens, each 155 × 169 cm., designated Important National Properties. Sambō-in, a subtemple of the Daigō-ji, Kyoto.

31. Ogata Kōrin, "Red and White Plum Blossoms" (*Kōhakubai-zu Byōbu*), early eighteenth century, a pair of two-panel screens, each 106 × 172 cm., designated National Treasures. Atami Art Museum, Shizuoka Prefecture.

Heian-period art. Sōtatsu was fond of compositions that developed diagonally across the painted surface, and the same emphasis on the diagonal is found in many parts of the Katsura Palace—examples are the zigzagged floor plan of the main building and the triangular patches of velvet in the Middle Room of the Shōi-ken.

Kōrin's art, while even more richly decorative than Sōtatsu's, is on the whole less sentimental and more coldly calculated. In his famous screen painting entitled "Red and White Plum Blossoms" (*Figure 31*) the emphasis is not on the striking colors, but on rounded shapes and curvilinear movement. Behind the superficial gorgeousness, there lurks a somewhat cynical taste for paradox and for purely intellectual amusement. One is reminded of the whimsical gourd-shaped window in the Second Room of the Shōkin-tei, of the "laughing windows" in the Shōi-ken, and of the design of a crescent moon alongside the sun in the remarkable Three Lights Lantern, which stands next to the boat mooring at the Shōi-ken. There is premeditated and to a degree defiant eccentricity in this use of intellectualized forms. One senses the aristocratic disdain felt by the well-bred men of letters in Kyoto for the ordinary world from which they had been alienated by shogunal decree. The use of such sophisticated symbolism in a country house presupposes taste for pleasures of a higher order than those enjoyed by the common herd.

No better illustration of this determination to rise high above it all can be seen than in the use of enormously expensive materials in seemingly modest designs. The Katsura shelving in the Imperial Dais, for example, is built of four or five varieties of exotic imported wood, while the innocent-looking veranda outside the Music Room is floored with beautifully grained and extremely costly cryptomeria planks. Similarly, the paper with the blue-and-white checkered design in the Shōkin-tei is of the highest quality made in Japan. One hesitates even to consider the cost of the countless rocks and unusual plants and trees in the garden. The Katsura Palace is, all in all, a triumph of symbolic decorativeness of a sort that could only be achieved by a well-educated Japanese aristocrat steeped in the culture of the past. This is not the "stately pleasure dome" of Kublai Khan, but rather a monument to the intellectual achievements and cultivated tastes of the contemporary nobility.

A Beautiful Dream

The word "katsura" refers to a tree of the *Cercidiphyllum* genus, but has connotations of a more romatic nature.

According to Chinese folklore, there was once a man who had learned the Taoist secret of immortality, but who had committed an offense that required severe punishment. He was therefore sentenced to go to the moon and spend the rest of eternity trying to chop down a five-thousand-foot katsura tree that could never be felled. The shadowy images that we see in the moon now are accordingly those of the condemned woodcutter and his tree. Because of this story, the katsura came to symbolize not only the moon, but also, by extension, a much

desired yet unattainable goal. A poem in the *Man'yōshū* says:

Oh, what shall I do
With this charming young damsel?
Though she can be seen,
Like the katsura in the moon,
She can never be taken.

The katsura tree brings to mind a land of fantasy, of moonlight and beautiful dreams—the sort of ephemeral, romantic world conjured up by the novels of the Heian period and no doubt treasured by such literary men as Prince Toshihito and Prince Noritada.

It is not known when or why the district in which the Katsura Palace is situated came to be known by this name. In ancient times, this was a part of Kadono County in the province of Yamashiro, which was first developed by a clan named Hata. The Hata are thought to have been of Chinese origin, and they may possibly have named the area Katsura after the tree that figures in the old Chinese katsura-in-the-moon story.* In any case, in the Heian period, this area was the site of a country house owned by the great regent Fujiwara no Michinaga and his son Yorimichi. The house is mentioned as the "Katsura Mansion" in the *Tale of Genji*, which was to some extent inspired by Michinaga's life. Aside from the lyrical connotations of the word "katsura," therefore, the Katsura area came to be known as the country seat of the greatest of all Fujiwara nobles. Katsura was thus both by name and tradition an eminently suitable place for Prince Toshihito to build his country retreat.

We have seen that he constructed the earlier version of the Katsura

* There is also a plant called the "vine katsura" (*tsutakazura*), which commonly grows wild in wooded areas, and it may be that the name Katsura was applied as a sort of pun to a district covered with this and other low plants. In this connection, it is worth noting that the Koryū-ji in Kyoto, which was the ancestral temple of the Hata family, was at one time known as the Keirin-ji, or "Temple of the Forest of Katsura Trees."

Palace around 1616, just after the battle of Osaka and the issuance of the seventeen-article Rules for the Imperial Court and the Nobility. It can easily be imagined that the prince felt the need for a place where he could enjoy a life free of the political intrigues of Kyoto and devote his time to reading, studying, and entertaining his friends. That the Katsura Palace is included in the "Scenes Inside and Outside the Capital" of 1615–18 indicates that it had already become well known by then. One is tempted to suppose that the courtiers and wealthy merchants who formed the cultural elite of Kyoto had come to regard it as a haven for their kind of people. Prince Toshihito's house, as we have seen, was not nearly as large or elaborate as the Katsura Palace is now, but his "teahouse in the melon patch" appears to have served him well as a pleasant sanctuary during the latter years of his life.

Three days before his death, he wrote a short will in which he urged his son to put scholarship before all else. Prince Noritada seems to have taken his father at his word, for only two months later he began studying under Kentaku of the Shōkoku-ji. In recording this event, the priest mentions that the young man was both quick and intelligent. Eventually the time came when he could turn his wit and sensibilities to the reconstruction and enlargement of the Katsura Palace.

Like the katsura in the moon, the palace and its garden have an unreal, fantastic quality. The visitor coming for the first time is troubled by a loss of orientation. This starts soon after he has crossed the Katsura River and turned north onto the road leading up by the river to the Front Gate. Though the road seems to lead north, it gradually shifts direction toward the west, so that by the time the visitor has passed the Katsura fencing and entered the compound, he is headed south. Unaware of the change, he has been drawn into a new set of coordinates completely backwards from those to which he is accustomed. Partly because of this, there are few people who can make

their way about the palace grounds without a guide; even with a guide, most visitors have trouble telling where they are without a map. It is rather like being in a maze. The architecture is of little assistance in this respect, for the main building, instead of facing south in the accepted Japanese style, is shifted sixty-three degrees to the east. The whole compound is a world unto itself, cut off even by its geography from tiresome reality.

The garden is a series of unexpected sights. Along the Imperial Pathway and through the Maple Riding Lane, the walk is paved with small flat rocks, but these give way, at the approach to the Outer Arbor, to large stepping stones, to the right of which one is astonished to see a grove of fern palms, seemingly transported in some mysterious fashion from an island in the South Seas. Directly in front of the Outer Arbor is a straight walk in which long slabs alternate with smaller rocks and pebbles in a most striking fashion. Instead of conducting one, as might be expected, to a building or some other impressive sight, this straight section comes to an abrupt end before a modest stone lantern, and one is forced to turn left. After a step or two, one comes upon the Rocky Shore, a small peninsula made to look like a windswept reef. Presently the path leads across the single-slab stone bridge to the Shōkin-tei, where, after taking in the rustic thatch roof, one is regaled by the distinctly modern blue-and-white checkered pattern of the paper on the sliding doors and the wall of the alcove. To recover from the tension caused by the series of shocks thus far experienced, at this point the visitor may pause in the unfloored loggia and look out over the pond at a variety of interesting sights, each of which is a photographer's dream. The walk then leads through the subdued Valley of Fireflies to the hillock on which stands the Shōka-tei, the little pavilion in the style of a mountainside teashop. Though the elevation here is a mere five meters, the gradual climb up a series of stepping stones gives the impression of a genuine mountain—a feeling enhanced by the view of the entire main house from the top. For the first time, the total spatial perspective becomes evident.

Throughout the garden thus far, visual delights have followed one upon another as though mounted on a revolving stage. Just as the visitor is about to lose himself in all this beauty, however, he is brought up short by the "laughing windows" of the Shōi-ken, which remind him that everything about Katsura is a feat of the intellect.

In contrast to the dynamic, constantly changing atmosphere of the garden, the interior space of the buildings, particularly the main house, is static in the extreme. When the visitor enters the Second Room of the Old Shoin, he is stopped cold by the stunning view out over the Moon-Viewing Platform toward the pond, which, from this vantage point, looks like a placid lake deep in the mountains. In the garden, the designer has developed his various themes by repeatedly shifting the line of vision, but inside, the viewer's position is fixed, and he becomes aware of subtle changes occurring outside—the movements of the mist in the morning, the variations in the light coming through the trees as the day progresses, the reflection of the moon dancing on the water at night. Where the dramatic shifting of scenery in the garden has made one oblivious to time, the quiet serenity of the house makes one hypersensitive to it. If only for that reason, the spatial gap between the house and the garden at Katsura seems enormous—an effect resulting directly from the fact that the building is raised to a very high level above the ground.

As a rule, Japanese residential architecture is distinguished by spatial continuity between interior and exterior, and at a glance one might be deceived by the outside corridors at Katsura into thinking that such interpenetration exists here. When the floors are as far off the ground as they are in this building, however, there is very little real connection between house and garden. This is especially true of the Middle Shoin and the New Palace, where the framing of the openings seems to mask off all but a portion of the exterior world. The effect is rather like that of a large television screen which reveals a realm different from the one in which we actually live. Just as in the case of a television tube, the view enclosed within the frame stimulates our imagination—we create for ourselves a whole cosmos of which the scene we see might be a part.

To go through the Katsura Palace and its garden is in many ways like seeing a good play, made all the better by the absence of anything conspicuously theatrical. The effects seem very natural; before the spectator realizes it, he has been drawn completely into a make-believe situation. In the course of Japanese architectural history, quite a few people have attempted to build imaginary worlds for themselves. An example in classical times was Fujiwara no Yorimichi's private temple, the Byōdō-in in Uji (*Figure 32*), which was deliberately designed to reproduce on earth the glories of the Western Paradise of the Buddha Amida. In the middle ages, Ashikaga Yoshimitsu attempted at his mansion outside Kyoto (*Figure 33*) to recreate the religious world he saw in the teachings of the great Zen master Musō Soseki. In both cases, the effect of otherworldly beauty was sought by placing in quasi-natural settings buildings of very lavish and artificial design— beautiful and ornate palaces of the sort that might be imagined to exist in heaven. To judge from the Phoenix Hall and the Golden Pavilion, which are all that remain of Yorimichi's and Yoshimitsu's extrava- ganzas, the results looked contrived. Most people would agree that the two buildings have a beauty of their own, but they also have a dramatic quality that prevents them from seeming quite real. Artifice calls attention to the imaginary nature of their design.

In a different way, the rustic Japanese teahouse, for all its efforts to appear simple and bucolic, is patently artificial. It requires no great

32. The Phoenix Hall, built in 1053, at the Byōdō-in, Uji.

33. The Golden Pavilion at the Rokuon-ji (Kinkaku-ji), Kyoto. Built c. 1398, rebuilt in 1955.

insight to perceive that the use of rare and expensive timbers in designs that are supposed to be rustic is essentially false. The Katsura Palace is not entirely free of such incongruities, but they are neither numerous nor conspicuous. The economy of design here creates clean, tidy spaces which entice the visitor into a world of dreams.

Bruno Taut's idea that the Katsura Palace represents the best in traditional Japanese architecture and the Tōshō-gū the worst has gained wide acceptance since his time. This view, it will be recalled, is linked with the notion that what was done by the emperor was meritorious, whereas what was done by the shogun was meretricious.

In comparing Katsura and Nikko, we should always keep in mind that they were constructed for entirely different purposes. If Katsura represents the world of the imaginary, Nikko is very much the world of the here and now. The Tōshō-gū was built for the express purpose of apotheosizing Tokugawa Ieyasu and thereby sanctifying the authority of the Tokugawa government. It was intended to overawe, not to furnish a locale for daydreams, and it had to be designed in such a way as to stress its monumentality as well as its costliness. In short, it was conceived as an expensive and impressive ornament; its elaborate decorations were essential to its function. Note, for example, that among the numerous sculptured designs that adorn the Karamon ("Chinese gate"), which may be regarded as typical of the architecture at Nikko, we find in a transom a panorama based on the story of the mythical Chinese emperor Shun-ti, who is a Confucian hero (*Figure 34*). This is a direct expression of the Tokugawa government's determination to force the ethics of Confucianism upon the common people. Similarly, the famous monkey motif signifying "hear no evil, speak no evil, see no evil" (*Figure 35*) was intended to impress on people the motto that they were expected to follow in a feudal society. Japanese of the Edo period understood the point perfectly.

It is a mistake, therefore, to think that Nikko is a product of bad taste on the part of the shogun who built it. The very same shogun, it

35. "Hear no evil, speak no evil, see no evil"—carving on a panel in the Sacred Stable at the Tōshō-gū, Nikko.

34. The transom on the Karamon ("Chinese Gate") at the Tōshō-gū in Nikko depicts the story of the mythical Chinese emperor, Shun-ti, a Confucian hero.

should be observed, employed Kobori Enshū to design a garden for Edo Castle that measured up to that of Katsura in its serene other-worldliness. If Katsura is to be taken as representative of that which is dreamlike and fabricative in Japanese architecture, then Nikko needs to be appraised from an entirely different angle.

The Momoyama period* in Japan has been compared with the European Renaissance, because it too was an age characterized by an upsurge of humanism and a revival of classical culture. Similarly, the period that immediately followed—the era during which the Nikko shrines were built—has been described as Baroque. Parallels of this sort are always to be regarded with caution, because they tend to ignore very real differences between Japanese and European society, but it cannot be denied that certain striking similarities arise from time to time. Specifically, the aesthetics of alienation or escape seen at Katsura—the pursuit of the idealized mountain-hut image, coupled

* It is difficult to assign specific dates to this age. From the political viewpoint, it can be limited to the period of Nobunaga and Hideyoshi, which is to say roughly from 1573 to 1600, but culturally it lingered on for another two or three decades.

with eclectic classicism and a strong emphasis on intellectuality—has a close spiritual counterpart in European Mannerism, which flourished between the High Renaissance and the Baroque age. The physical resemblance may be negligible, but we see in Katsura the same rejection of the real and insistence upon ideal beauty over actuality.

The latter part of the Edo period is singularly lacking in outstanding structures. It is almost as though architecture had been forgotten in an excess of carpentry. Yet even in this age, the architecture of reality seen in the Tōshō-gū remained an attraction that the people visited and admired. "Never say 'perfect' until you've seen Nikkō" became a proverb known to every Japanese man, woman, and child. And what of Katsura? As we have already seen, it was forgotten: by the early Meiji period, soldiers were using it as a hideaway, unconscious of its architectural meaning. Furthermore, if Bruno Taut had not pointed out its merit to the Japanese intelligentsia of his time, it may well have remained forgotten, or nearly so. Certainly it would not have acquired the fame and admiration it enjoys today.

No matter how beautiful architecture may be, it is essentially mundane and materialistic. Buildings must be real, in the sense that they must have some definite connection with the society of their period. The Katsura Palace, being an imaginary fabrication, to a large extent denies this aspect of architecture, and for that reason it passed into oblivion for more than a century. It was a flower blooming out of season, and in its continuous refinement of form and thought, it was just as fragile as the works of the Mannerists in sixteenth-century Europe. Still, as a search for ideal delights within the very concrete medium of architecture, the Katsura Palace may be regarded as one of the most avant-garde creations in the history of Japanese art. Because of its deliberate tenseness, thoroughgoing subjectivity, and emphasis on keen-wittedness, it remains a beautiful world of dreams.

CHRONOLOGY
GENEALOGY
PLATE NOTES

CHRONOLOGY

1535 Lower Katsura demesne became part of the estate of the Konoe family.

1573 Hosokawa Fujitaka (later called Yūsai; 1534–1610) received in grant from Nobunaga those parts of Yamashiro Province (Kyoto Prefecture) lying west of the Katsura River.

1579 Prince Toshihito was born. The sixth son of Prince Sanehito, he was named Kosamaru at birth.

1588 Emperor Go-Yōzei (1571–1617) visited Hideyoshi at the Jurakudai, where the feudal lords were summoned to greet him.
Kosamaru became Hideyoshi's adopted son.

1590 The collateral imperial house of Hachijō was established.

1591 Kosamaru was given the name Prince Toshihito by imperial order.

1596 Prince Toshihito studied *renga* (linked verse) under Hosokawa Yūsai.

1597 Kobori Sakusuke (usually called Masakazu, Lord of Enshū, or simply Enshū; 1579–1647) married the adopted daughter of Lord Tōdō of Izumi.

1598 The Hachijō estate in Ishida, Ogurusu, and Kobata was replaced with nine villages in Funai County, Tamba Province.

1600 Prince Toshihito received a diploma from Hosokawa Yūsai in the study of the *Anthology of Ancient and Modern Poetry (Kokin Wakashū)*.

1601 Prince Toshihito was promoted to the first order of imperial princes.

1602 Prince Toshihito had a well dug and a teahouse built in the Hachijō residence in Kyoto.

1605 The Imperial Palace compound was enlarged to the north, and the Hachijō residence was moved to Imadegawa Avenue.

1606 Prince Toshihito went to Osaka Castle to thank Toyotomi Hideyori (1593–1615) for construction work of some sort.

1609 A new *shoin* was constructed at the Hachijō residence in Imadegawa.

1612 Prince Toshihito made a sightseeing tour of Amanohashidate and Waka-sanoura in Tango Province (northern part of Kyoto Prefecture).

1616 Proposal was made for the marriage of Prince Toshihito to Lady Sen (1597–1666), the daughter of Tokugawa Hidetada (1579–1632) and widow of Toyotomi Hideyori.
Prince Toshihito went to Senshō-ji to "view his melons" and "take a walk about Katsura."
The consort of the ex-Emperor Go-Yōzei paid a visit to Katsura.
Prince Toshihito was married to the daughter of Kyōgoku Takatomo (1572–1622).

1617 Prince Toshihito went to Edo, where the shogun, Hidetada, confirmed his holdings in Lower Katsura and other places in the same area "as before."

1619 The affair of the imperial concubine Oyotsu became known.
Prince Noritada was born and named Takomaro.

1620 Prince Toshihito's mother, Shinjō Tōmon'in, died.
A teahouse was constructed at Lower Katsura.

1621 Princess Ume, daughter of Prince Toshihito, was born.

1622 A second son was born to Prince Toshihito. He was later to become the Priestly Imperial Prince Ryōshō.

1624 A third son was born to Prince Toshihito. Named Sachimaru at first, he was later to become Hirohata Tadayuki.
The priest Kentaku, of the Shōkoku-ji, visited the country house in Katsura.

1625 Prince Toshihito made a second visit to Edo.
The priest Sūden, of the Konchi-in, wrote the *Record of the Katsura Pavilion (Katsura-tei-ki)*.
Prince Toshihito gave lessons in the *Anthology of Ancient and Modern Poetry (Kokin Wakashū)* to Emperor Go-Mizunoo.

1628 The Buddhist nun Keisen of the Daishō-ji visited the Katsura house.

1629 Coming-of-age ceremony was held for Prince Noritada.
Prince Toshihito died at the age of fifty.

1631 Kentaku went to the Katsura house and was surprised at its dilapidation.

1632 Prince Noritada made a trip to Edo.

1633 There was a large typhoon in the Kyoto region, and the great bridge over the Yodo River was washed away.

1634 Prince Noritada was received by the shogun, Tokugawa Iemitsu (1604–1651), at Nijō Castle in Kyoto.
Prince Toshihito's second son entered the Buddhist clergy and was given the name Ryōshō Hōshinnō (the Priestly Imperial Prince Ryōshō).

1635 There was a large typhoon in the Kyoto region.

1636 Kanō Uneme Morinobu (1602–1674) was given the priestly title *Hōgen* (Eye of the Law) and the name Tan'yū.

1637 Prince Noritada invited his uncle, the Priestly Imperial Prince Ryōjo, to his teahouse (*sukiya*) at the Imadegawa residence.

1640 Princess Ume was married to Ryōjo of the Hongan-ji (a different person from the Ryōjo who was Prince Toshihito's brother).

1641 The three Kanō brothers, Tan'yū, Yasunobu, and Naonobu, painted door paintings for the Imperial Palace. The Middle Shoin at Katsura was built around this time.

1642 Prince Noritada married Lady Fū (Ofū), the daughter of Maeda Toshitsune (1593–1658). Iemitsu gave Prince Noritada 300 pieces of silver and other articles as a wedding present.

1643 Prince Yasuhito was born. The ninth son of ex-Emperor Go-Mizunoo, he was first known as Prince Sachi.
The Priestly Imperial Prince Ryōjo died.

1645 Prince Noritada went to Katsura with his brother, Sachimaru.
Prince Noritada made his second trip to Edo.

1646 Ryōshō became abbot of the Tendai Sect.
Around this time, Prince Noritada went to Sakai and saw teahouses designed by Sen no Rikyū.

1648 Princess Ume died at the age of twenty-seven.

1649 Priests Ganryō, Hōrin Shōshō, and others, of the Konchi-in, visited Katsura. There were five teahouses at the time.

1650 Prince Toshihito's third son, Sachimaru, came of age and was betrothed to the daughter of Tokugawa Yoshinao (1600–1650), Lord of Owari.

1651 Ryōshō made a trip to Edo.

1654 Prince Sachi, son of Go-Mizunoo, was adopted by Prince Noritada.

1655 Prince Sachi moved to the Hachijō residence and was given the name Prince Yasuhito.
Ex-Emperor Go-Sai's first son, later to become Prince Osahito, was born.

1656 Ryōshō built the Manju-in in Kyoto.

1657 Prince Noritada was promoted to the second order of imperial princes.
Prince Noritada's steward, Chūjō Sakyō was summoned to the shogunate and made a direct vassal of the shogun.

1658 Ex-Emperor Go-Mizunoo visited the Katsura Palace.

1661 There was a great fire in Kyoto, and the Hachijō residence burned down. The shogun made a grant of 200 *kan* of silver to Prince Yasuhito.

1662 Prince Noritada died at the age of forty-three.

1663 Ex-Emperor Go-Mizunoo visited the Katsura Palace twice.

1664 Prince Sachimaru took the surname Hirohata.

1665 Prince Yasuhito died at the age of twenty-two.

1666 The first son of ex-Emperor Go-Sai was appointed heir to Prince Yasuhito.

1667 The new heir moved to the Hachijō residence.

1669 The new heir was given the name Prince Osahito.
Hirohata Tadayuki died at the age of forty-five.
Jōshō-in, Prince Toshihito's widow, died.

1671 Ex-Emperor Go-Sai's ninth son, later to become Prince Hisahito, was born.

1675 Prince Osahito died at the age of twenty.

1679 Karasuyama Suketada, who wrote the character for "moon" for the door fittings of that form in the New Palace, died.

1680 The sixth son of Emperor Reigen, later to become Prince Ayahito, was born.

1684 The ninth son of ex-Emperor Go-Sai was given the name Prince Hisahito.

1689 Emperor Reigen's eighth son, later called Prince Saku, was born.
Kobori Jin'emon Masanori saw the Katsura Palace.
Prince Hisahito died at the age of eighteen.

1692 Prince Saku died at the age of three.

1696 The sixth son of Emperor Reigen was made heir to the Hachijō estate, and the name of the family was changed to Kyōgoku.

1697 The new heir was named Prince Ayahito.

1703 Prince Ayahito had a son who later became Prince Yakahito.

1708 Prince Ayahito's residence (formerly the Hachijō residence) in Kyoto burned. The whole village of Katsura was flooded; the Shōkin-tei and other buildings in the Katsura Palace were damaged.

1709 Prince Ayahito's son was given the name Prince Yakahito.

1710 Prince Ayahito died at the age of thirty.

1717 Fujimoto Sōhachirō, a retainer of the Kobori family, drew a picture of the Outer Arbor and its stone toilet.

1721 Floodwater came up under the floor of the Shōkin-tei.

1733 Lord Kobori of Bichū (later Lord of Izumi) was given a wooden model of a water basin near the Outer Arbor, said to have been made by Kobori Enshū. Prince Yakahito had a son who later became Prince Kinhito.

1745 Prince Kinhito was given his name by imperial decree.

1753 Prince Kinhito went to the Katsura Palace.

1754 Prince Yakahito went with Fukimaru of the Chion-in and Bishop Jinkei of the Kakua-in to Katsura.

1755 Prince Yakahito went with his consort and Prince Kinhito to Katsura.

1759 Prince Yakahito went to Katsura.

1767 Prince Yakahito died at the age of sixty-four.

1770 Prince Kinhito died at the age of thirty-seven.

1788 There was a great fire in Kyoto and the Kyōgoku family's residence burned.

1810 Emperor Kōkaku's fourth son, Prince Iwa, who was later to become Prince Takehito, was born.
The name of the Kyōgoku family was changed to Katsura.

1811 Prince Iwa was named Prince Takehito by imperial decree. He died in the same year.

1828 A daughter named Princess Toshi, later to become Princess Sumiko, was born to Emperor Ninkō.

1833 Emperor Ninkō's sixth son, Prince Miki, who was later to become Prince Misahito, was born.

1835 Prince Miki was named head of the Katsura family.

1836 Prince Miki was named Prince Misahito by imperial decree. He died in the same year.

1842 Princess Toshi was named Imperial Princess Sumiko.

1862 Princess Sumiko became head of the house of Katsura.

1870 Princess Sumiko was given an allowance of 1,015 *koku*.

1871 The property on which the Katsura Palace stands was granted to the house of Katsura.

1873 Princess Sumiko's allowance was terminated, and she was given a grant of 6,800 yen.

1881 Princess Sumiko died at the age of fifty-three.

1884 The Katsura Palace was put under the jurisdiction of the Imperial Household Ministry.

1934 Bruno Taut saw the Katsura Palace and wrote praises of it. After this it acquired worldwide fame as an example of Japanese architecture.

GENEALOGY of the Hachijō-Kyōgoku-Katsura Line

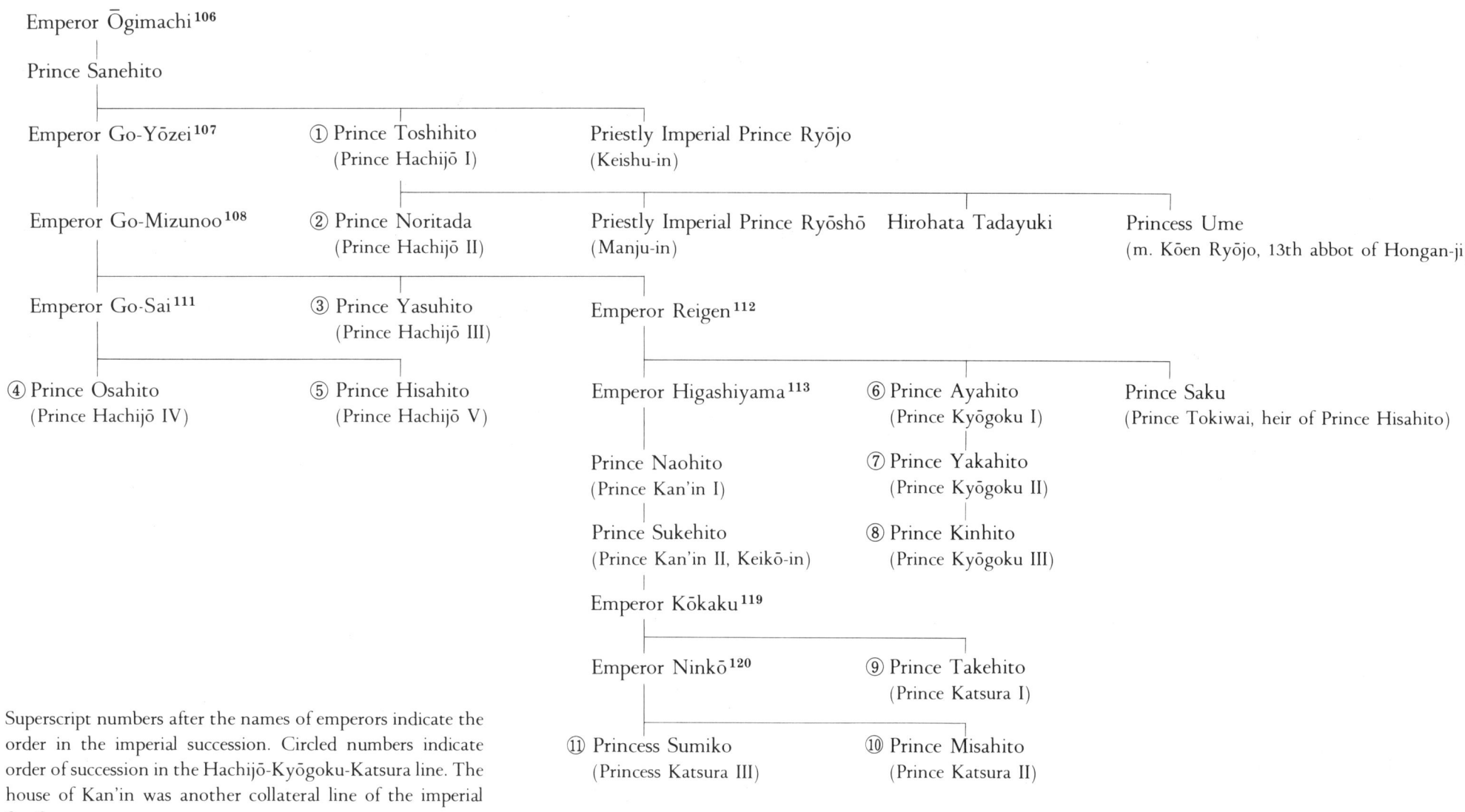

Emperor Ōgimachi[106]

Prince Sanehito

Emperor Go-Yōzei[107]　①Prince Toshihito　Priestly Imperial Prince Ryōjo
(Prince Hachijō I)　(Keishu-in)

Emperor Go-Mizunoo[108]　②Prince Noritada　Priestly Imperial Prince Ryōshō　Hirohata Tadayuki　Princess Ume
(Prince Hachijō II)　(Manju-in)　(m. Kōen Ryōjo, 13th abbot of Hongan-ji)

Emperor Go-Sai[111]　③Prince Yasuhito　Emperor Reigen[112]
(Prince Hachijō III)

④Prince Osahito　⑤Prince Hisahito　Emperor Higashiyama[113]　⑥Prince Ayahito　Prince Saku
(Prince Hachijō IV)　(Prince Hachijō V)　(Prince Kyōgoku I)　(Prince Tokiwai, heir of Prince Hisahito)

Prince Naohito　⑦Prince Yakahito
(Prince Kan'in I)　(Prince Kyōgoku II)

Prince Sukehito　⑧Prince Kinhito
(Prince Kan'in II, Keikō-in)　(Prince Kyōgoku III)

Emperor Kōkaku[119]

Emperor Ninkō[120]　⑨Prince Takehito
(Prince Katsura I)

Superscript numbers after the names of emperors indicate the
order in the imperial succession. Circled numbers indicate
order of succession in the Hachijō-Kyōgoku-Katsura line. The
house of Kan'in was another collateral line of the imperial
family.

⑪Princess Sumiko　⑩Prince Misahito
(Princess Katsura III)　(Prince Katsura II)

PLATE NOTES

THE KATSURA RIVER AND
THE IMPERIAL PATHWAY

The Katsura River is part of a stream that originates in the mountains northwest of Kyoto and descends in a series of rapids and falls through the valley between Mount Arashi and Mount Ogura. When it reaches the plain below, it spreads out into a steady flow, which in the Edo period (1603–1868) was broad and voluminous enough to be called the "Great Katsura River." When the Katsura Palace was still the country home of the Hachijō princes, there was no bridge over the river, and visitors had to approach by boat (*Figure 36*).

1 Katsura fencing

On the east border of the palace grounds is a fence composed of living black bamboo, woven together in such a way as to appear to be a natural growth. It is typical of traditional Japanese design that nature is not rigidly forced into artificial patterns, as in the stately formal gardens of Europe, but merely nudged, as it were, into forms that serve a practical or aesthetic purpose without losing their natural look. Where the Western designer imposed a human will upon nature, the Japanese designer attempted to conform with it, or at least to seem to conform (*Figure 37*). In effect, the Japanese designer *created* nature in an image that suited his needs. This principle is evident throughout the design of Katsura Palace and its garden. The bamboo hedge seen here is widely known as "Katsura fencing" (*Katsuragaki*).

36. Aerial view of the Katsura Palace and garden.

37. A view of the inner side of the Katsura fencing, clearly showing its construction.

2 Bamboo-sprig fencing

At the north end of the Katsura fencing, the road turns to the west. From this point to the Front Gate (*Plate 3*), the more elaborate and artificial type of fencing seen here is employed for the purpose of emphasizing the frontality. The thick bamboo posts are buried in the ground, and their tops are sliced off diagonally so as to bring out the distinction between inside and outside. The horizontal pieces are sprigs of bamboo, tied to the posts at intervals with hemp-palm rope. This type of fencing is known to Japanese gardeners as "bamboo-sprig fencing" (*takehogaki*).

3 The Front Gate

The Front Gate, which is the main entrance to the palace grounds, is slightly recessed from the plane of the bamboo-sprig fencing. The design could hardly be simpler: two heavy logs serve as gateposts, and the door leaves, as well as the fencing immediately to the right and left, are made of polished bamboo, set vertically in the framing. The neatness and regularity of the pattern stand out conspicuously in the natural green surroundings. The gate used today by ordinary visitors is farther along to the right, beyond an earth-covered bridge.

4 The Imperial Gate

Inside the Front Gate, a straight pathway lined on either side with pine trees continues for a distance of about sixty meters to the Imperial Gate, so called because it is thought to have been built for the use of the ex-Emperor Go-Mizunoo when he visited the palace in 1663. Ordinarily, gateways built specially for the use of an imperial personage are of relatively florid design, but here the emphasis is on the "mountain-hut" aspect of the palace.

5 Detail of the roof of the Imperial Gate

The two posts, as well as the ridge pole and outer beams, are unstripped cork oak logs—a type of wood not normally considered good enough for use in Japanese architecture. The emphasis on the rustic is enhanced by the thatched roof and the bamboo used for the structural parts of the ceiling.

6 The Imperial Gate viewed from inside the garden

Within the Imperial Gate is the Imperial Pathway, a stretch of about forty meters leading to the right. This is lined on both sides with maple trees, behind which are walls of shrubbery cut to about eye level. The leaves of the gate are grilles made from strips of split bamboo. Once inside this passageway, one feels completely cut off from the outside world.

7–8 Pebble pavement of the Imperial Pathway

To ensure proper drainage, the pebbles are embedded in the clay to only about half their height. Moss growing in the cracks combines with the blue-black hue of the pebbles to form a mosaiclike texture of startling beauty.

9 Detail of the earthen wall by the Imperial Pathway

This rustic creation stands to the right of the Imperial Pathway, near the point where the pathway comes to an end. To the left of the wall is a lane leading to the Ordinary Gate, which today is the entranceway for sightseers. Though the design of the wall seems unstudied, the subtle color relationship between the textured red clay and the green surroundings produces patterns that shift constantly with the season and the climate. The yellowish tinge that occurs when light falls on the wall through the trees in late autumn accords with the wistful, lonely atmosphere considered appropriate for a "mountain hut."

10 Earthen wall by the Imperial Pathway

Here the wall shown in Plate 9 is seen on a cloudy day in early spring. There is a fresh reddish cast that only hints at the brightness of the season, while at the same time imparting a sense of restraint and quiet good taste.

11 The Sumiyoshi Pine

At the end of the Imperial Pathway, the walk turns to the left, and a planting of shrubbery on either side focuses one's vision on a rather small, carefully shaped pine tree standing at the tip of a miniature cape. The emphasis on perspective imparts a dramatic effect, pictorial in nature, yet somehow at variance with the principles of traditional Japanese painting. Drawn closer by the psychological attraction, one sees for the first time the panorama of the pond and the Shōkin-tei beyond it. This is a landscape design of dazzling brilliance, perhaps the most spectacular in the whole Katsura compound. Formerly there was, on a reef to the left, another tree, the Takasago Pine, which formed a pair with the Sumiyoshi Pine. Pine trees bearing the same names—Takasago and Sumiyoshi—are referred to in the preface of the *Anthology of Ancient and Modern Poetry* (*Kokin Wakashū*), an imperial poetry collection on which the first two Hachijō princes were considered to be authorities.

INTERIOR OF THE MAIN HOUSE

The main house of the Katsura Palace consists of three sections, known as the Old Shoin, the Middle Shoin, and the New Palace. These are strung out on a zigzag plan, which makes possible broad openings on the east and south sides in all three apartments. The house as a whole faces the large garden pond to the east.

The Old Shoin is thought to be a revised version of the "little teahouse in the melon patch" built around 1616 by Prince Toshihito, the first head of the Hachijō family. The Middle Shoin was added by Prince Toshihito's heir, Prince Noritada, around 1641, at which time the Old Shoin was reconstructed in its present form. The New Palace appears to have been built in about 1655, when Prince Sachi, a son of the ex-Emperor Go-Mizunoo, was appointed heir to the Hachijō line. After Prince Sachi actually succeeded as head of the family, under the name Prince Yasuhito,

the New Palace was repaired and changed to some extent, most likely in 1663, when Go-Mizunoo made two formal progresses to Katsura.

The three sections of the main house reflect the shift from the *shoin* style of the late middle ages to the *sukiya* style of the early Edo period—a historical transition that led to the development of modern Japanese residential architecture.

12 The Central Gate

The main house is approached through this gate, which, like the Imperial Gate (*Plates 4 and 5*), is a simple structure with a thatched roof. The gate differs from the Imperial Gate in having auxiliary posts before and behind the two principal gateposts. Because of this, it is known as a "four-poster gate" (*yotsuashimon*). Although it is the most formal gate in the palace compound, its style is distinctly rustic; the posts are polished cryptomeria logs, the doors are made of thin cryptomeria planks, and the roof is thatched. Through the opening in the gate one can see the railing of the "Tiger Veranda," so called because it has a wooden door on which there is a painting of a tiger, attributed to Kanō Eitoku. This veranda is next to the Entrance Hall.

Also visible here is a tall stone water basin, which is the only prominent ornament in the area. Resembling a memorial stone in shape and size, the basin, though large, is almost completely expressionless. The cold, impersonal effect of the scene framed by the gate creates an impression of dignity and solemnity, which tend to inspire hesitancy and doubt on the part of the visitor.

13 Footpath in front of the Entrance Hall

A stone-paved walk leads at an angle across the yard from the Central Gate to the steps of the Entrance Hall. The direction of approach is almost due south, which is to say opposite from the normal direction (as noted elsewhere, Japanese houses generally face south). The walk, which is 9.4 meters long and 75 centimeters wide, is paved with 44 cut-granite rocks, fitted together in accordance with an intricate design. The effect of this man-made

38. General view of the footpath to the Entrance Hall. The opening in the wall is an entrance to the garden.

pattern (*Figure 38*) is all the more startling because the emphasis to this point has been almost entirely on natural beauty.

This design was attributed at a rather early date to the great garden designer Kobori Enshū. In fact, it even came to be called the "true stone paving in the style of Enshū," the word "true" here signifying formal, proper, unabbreviated, as in the case of the standard noncursive forms of Chinese characters in calligraphy.

There is a passing resemblance between the arrangement of the rocks in this walk and that seen in Japanese castle walls, but the bold ornamentalization of the design shows an aesthetic sensitivity that seems more modern than traditional. The brilliance of this patterned composition stands in strong contrast to the austerity of the scene immediately inside the Central Gate.

14 Stone steps at the Entrance Hall

The Entrance Hall (*mikoshiyose*) was an architectural form used in proper aristocratic houses of the Heian period and afterward. The Japanese name signifies the place to which palanquins arriving from without were brought, for this was the entrance for honored guests, who could be expected to ride rather than walk.

At the end of the "true stone paving" shown in Plate 13, four steps lead up to the entrance, in front of which there is a large additional stone step called the "footgear stone." This was where guests removed their wooden clogs or straw sandals before entering the house.

The "footgear stone" is the visual terminal of the "true stone paving" and may be regarded as part of the same overall design. The massive rock is 2.3 meters long and 78 centimeters wide. It has a roughly chipped finish and is shaped so that the center is 3 centimeters higher than the ends. The purpose no doubt was to prevent water from accumulating on the top, but the resulting nonrectangular corners may be seen as a deliberate deformation intended to contrast with the straightness of the path. After one passes this point, one is drawn into the interior by the white paper-covered doors on the other side of the veranda.

15 View of the garden from the Second Room of the Old Shoin

The Old Shoin functioned as a place in which guests could be formally received. It was consequently provided with a spectacular view of the garden—a sight much more dazzling than the interior of the building itself. The effect is all the more striking because, save for the one point along the approach where it can be glimpsed beyond the Sumiyoshi Pine, the garden is concealed until one enters this room and comes full upon it. A decorative framing for the outdoor scene is provided by the white paper-covered shoji.

16 The pond seen in winter across the Moon-Viewing Platform

On the east side of the Old Shoin, there is a spacious veranda beyond which extends a bamboo platform for viewing the moon. Ordinarily, Japanese houses face south, but in order to provide a view of the moon at Katsura, the building is shifted sixty-three degrees to the east. One is reminded of the large open verandas seen in pictures of Heian-period palaces, and it seems probable that the designer was deliberately aiming at the romantic spirit embodied in such classic literary works as the *Tale of Genji*. It is not difficult to visualize elegant noblemen in voluminous Heian-period robes looking out over the surface of the water and growing quietly ecstatic over the shimmering reflection of the moon. On a snowy day, time seems almost to freeze as one gazes out at the black and white patterns of the garden. One is transported to a world of Oriental ink landscapes, a realm of dreams in which the senses are lulled into blissful complacency.

17 Tokonoma in the First Room of the Old Shoin seen from the Second Room

As the most important room in the Old Shoin, the First Room is provided with a tokonoma. The principal post of the alcove, which is to say the one at the outer corner, is a cryptomeria log planed in such a way as to leave the bark on at the corners. All other posts visible in the picture are cryptomeria timbers cut to a size of 11.8 centimeters square. Four posts, including the two next to the principal post of the tokonoma, are made of wood having a straight grain on all sides, but since the wood has been stained, the lines do not stand out conspicuously. The tatami are of the size prevalent in Kyoto, 1.91 by .95 meters, and are bordered with dark blue linen cloth. The transom is simple and somewhat antique in appearance. Smaller wall panels are of plain white plaster, while the interior sliding doors, as well as the wall panels of the tokonoma, are covered with white paper bearing an ochre design of paulownia leaves, which attests to the imperial status of the Hachijō family. The Old Shoin differs in a number of respects from the classical *shoin* style and may be considered to represent a very early stage in the transition from that style to the *sukiya* style.

18 Tokonoma in the Third Room of the Middle Shoin

The Middle Shoin is entered by way of a room with a hearth (*Figure 39*), just behind the First Room of the Old Shoin. The floor of this apartment is set at a higher level to separate it from the Old Shoin, for this is a more private part of the house—in effect, the master's own living quarters. The Third Room was used for dining, and the connection with the Hearth Room and the pantry in the rear of the Old Shoin is therefore functional.

Shown in the plate is the inner (west) side of the main room in the Middle Shoin, known as the Third Room. The tokonoma is reminiscent of tearoom architecture, as is the recessed section with a lower ceiling on the right. The Third Room is also called the "Snow Room," because the paintings on the walls and doors, by Kanō Yasunobu, show birds flying among snow-laden reeds.

19 Tokonoma in the First Room of the Middle Shoin

Whereas the Old Shoin, as the place for entertaining guests, is relatively open and formal, the Middle Shoin, which served as the master's private apartment, has a quieter, more personal atmosphere. In the Edo period, apartments of this sort were given the generic name "black *shoin*" because of their generally subdued decor and lack of ostentation. At Katsura, we find that the paintings on the walls and door panels of the Middle Shoin are all black and white monochromes of a kind that would have appealed to Prince Noritada's fondness for study and the quiet life. Noteworthy among them is the landscape in the First Room, which occupies a tokonoma wall 3.8 meters wide, but consists mostly of a white background, with only the suggestion of a mountainous setting. The artist was Kanō Tan'yū, who is considered the greatest painter of his time. Tan'yū was also commissioned to make paintings for a number of other important architectural works, including Edo Castle, Nijō Castle, the Imperial Palace, and the Tōshō-gū in Nikko. The First Room of the Middle Shoin is also called the "Landscape Room" because of the painting.

20 Shelves in the First Room of the Middle Shoin

This arrangement of shelves is to the right of the landscape painting shown in Plate 19. Although situated in *sukiya*-style surroundings, the ensemble is a reversion to the classical *shoin* style. It is a design of great dignity and clarity, immaculate in both conception and execution. Painted on the four small doors of the uppermost cabinet are pictures of bamboo, the cotton rose, a narcissus, and chrysanthemums. The cloisonné handles of the door panels are said to have been made by Kachō, a well-known metalworker.

21 The veranda south of the Music Room

The Music Room, which is southwest of the Middle Shoin in the staggered plan, was the place where flutes, Japanese harps, lutes, and other musical instruments were stored. On its south side there is a wide veranda looking out over a broad expanse of lawn. The top rails are polished cryptomeria logs. Typical of the many small touches to be seen at Katsura are the little round knobs on the tops of the nails fixing the cross-pieces to the posts—a small circular element in an otherwise starkly rectangular silhouette.

39. Hearth Room in the Middle Shoin.

40. Detail of Ogata Kōrin's "Red and White Plum Blossoms," left panel of the right screen (cf. Figure 31, page 128).

22–23 Floor and railing of the veranda south of the Music Room

The boards of the floor have been washed time and again to bring out the grain. The resulting relief pattern is simple, but very decorative, calling to mind the clear flow of a brook in the mountains. There is a suggestion here of the stream in Ogata Kōrin's "Red and White Plum Blossoms" (*Figure 40*), and one is reminded that Ogata, too, strove to revive the beauty of classic Japanese art. This loving attention to small details is typical of *sukiya*-style architecture.

24 The Imperial Dais in the First Room of the New Palace

From the southwest end of the veranda beside the Music Room one enters the New Palace, which is the westernmost section of the main house. Though first constructed in the mid 1650s, this apartment was remodeled on the occasion of the ex-Emperor Go-Mizunoo's visit to the palace in the spring of 1663 and is more richly decorated than the Old Shoin or the Middle Shoin. It is particularly valuable as an example of the *sukiya* style during its best period. Nothing more clearly illustrates this style than the Imperial Dais, where a whole world of craftsmanship and design has been epitomized within the limited space of three tatami mats.

The ceiling, which consists of a black-lacquered frame with panels of *keyaki* wood, is set at a low level, and the floor is raised above that of the rest of the room, the step-up being made of horse-chestnut boards. The tatami are trimmed with a figured cloth known as "Korean edging," which was used in Heian-period palace architecture. To the left of the two front tatami, opening on the southwest, is a *shoin* window, the upper framing of which is in the pattern of a Japanese comb. Beside the window are a cabinet and shelves that turn at the corner of the room and continue along the west wall. This is famous in Japan as "Katsura shelving" or "true shelving." In contrast to the flowing lines of Kanō Tan'yū's monochrome ink paintings on five of the cabinet door panels, the arrangement of the cabinets and shelves creates geometrical pat-

terns reminiscent of Mondrian.

The materials used here are rosewood, ebony, and Chinese mulberry, none of which are native to Japan. It is characteristic of *sukiya* houses that expensive materials of this sort are apt to be employed in a reticent and unostentatious fashion. Though the design here is not, as legend would have it, by Kobori Enshū, it is nevertheless a prime example of the style favored in the age when his influence was strongest.

25 Cabinets in the Dressing Room of the New Palace

The Dressing Room is a cubicle directly behind the Imperial Dais where the ex-emperor's ladies waited when they were in attendance. Since these cabinets and shelves were on the north side of the east wall of the room, back to back with those of the Imperial Dais, they are often called the "back Katsura shelving." They too display a complicated pattern of geometrical shapes. The door panels of the cabinet are adorned with paintings by Kanō Tan'yū: landscapes with people, a sparrow amid bamboo twigs, orchids, plum blossoms, chrysanthemums, and peonies.

26 Room with the Imperial Washstand

The Room with the Imperial Washstand, which is behind the Dressing Room, is the anteroom of the toilet. Since it was a place where water might be sloshed about, its floor was made of split-bamboo slats. Seen on the right in the picture is a sunken water drain; at center is a four-pronged stand for a water bucket. It is a measure of the maturity of the *sukiya* style that close attention was paid to the design of everyday functional objects like these.

27 Door fitting modeled on the character for "moon"

Handles of this design are used on the door panels in the First Room and Second Room of the New Palace. They are meant to suggest the idea of the katsura tree in the moon (*see page 129*) and, by extension, to remind the visitor that the palace is situated in an ideal place for moon-viewing. Apart from the visual excellence of the design, it should be observed that these fittings are in line with the emphasis on conceptualism seen throughout the Katsura Palace. We are shown not a picture of the moon, but a written character meaning "moon," which recalls literary associations rather than lyrical visions. These handles are said to have been made by the famous metal craftsman Kachō.

28 Door fitting in the form of a pine needle

Handles of this design are employed on the sliding panels of the Music Room. The importance of pine trees in Japanese garden design requires no comment here, but it should be noted that this seemingly casual portrayal of a fallen pine leaf with one of its needles bent suggests the poignancy of autumn and the decline the season symbolizes. Both the pine-leaf motif and the design of a woman's traveling hat (*Figure 41*), employed for the fittings on the wooden doors between the Music Room and the Middle Shoin, may be regarded as symbolic of feminine sentiments.

29 Door fitting in the form of a vase of flowers

Door fixtures in the form of vases containing flowers of the four seasons are found on the wooden doors at the entrance to the New Palace. Spring is represented by cherry blossoms and wisteria; summer, by cotton roses and eulalia; fall, by chrysanthemums; and winter, by plum blossoms, camellias, and narcissuses. This photograph shows the winter design, which, together with the others in this series, suggests the constant changing of the seasons, with a hint of the carefree pleasures of the bucolic life. Though these handles are said to have been created by Gotō Sukenori, a metal craftsman of the Muromachi period (1338–1573), the ascription is not certain.

30 Nail concealer in the form of a narcissus

Like many other metal ornaments in the Katsura Palace, the one shown here is employed to conceal the unsightly head of a nail. In this case, the nail is one of those used to attach a horizontal board called a *nageshi* to the posts of a room in the New Palace. (A *nageshi* is a sort of frieze rail attached to the posts at the height of the upper door railing. It has no structural function, but is considered *de rigueur* in formal rooms. Though absent in the Old Shoin and Middle Shoin, it is employed in the First and Second Rooms of the New Palace because they were intended for the use of an exalted personage, the ex-Emperor Go-Mizunoo.) The narcissus pattern, though horizontal rather than vertical, is of essentially the same inspiration as the seasonal flowers found on the door fittings at the entrance to the New Palace (*Plate 29*). It was doubtless intended to set a tone of grace and elegance for the ex-emperor's visit. At the same time, it may be regarded as another of the minute refinements that characterize *sukiya*-style houses. The ornament is said to have been made by Kachō.

31 The veranda of the First Room in the New Palace

The floor level throughout the main house is unusually high off the ground, and the verandas serve as intermediary spaces between interior and exterior. Yet here, as in the Middle Shoin, the orientation of these outer corridors is inward, for the shoji and rain shutters are slid into place on the outer posts, and the tatami continue from the interior out onto the veranda floor. (Here the tatami extend only halfway across, but in the Middle Shoin, they run to the outer posts of the veranda.) The top rails of the bannister, which are octagonal in section, are adorned with metal fittings bearing a chrysanthemum arabesque. Curving panels are attached to the bannister posts to create a decorative framing. Bordering and containing the tatami are two long single-piece *keyaki* timbers, lacquered black. In fine weather, when the doors and shutters can be left open, interior and exterior are linked in a fashion that is peculiar to Japanese architecture.

41. Door fitting in the shape of a woman's hat.

EXTERIOR OF THE MAIN HOUSE

After seeing the New Palace, the visitor returns to the Old Shoin. From there, it is possible to go directly into the garden from exits on the northeast, southeast, and southwest sides. The usual procedure, however, is to go back to the small garden before the Entrance Hall and to enter the main garden through a rather low opening in a clay wall to the right (*Figure 38*). From the garden one can view the history of the main house as it progressed on its zigzag course from Old Shoin to New Palace.

32 Garden entrance seen from the garden side
Going through the garden entrance, which forces one to stoop slightly, has the effect of abstracting the thoughts and perspectives one has formed thus far. One anticipates the new vistas that are to open up ahead, but at the same time one is moved to take a reluctant look backward. The small opening is a whimsical device of the designer, intended to have the effect of combining expectancy with regret.

33 Exit at the northeast corner of the Old Shoin
As the visitor proceeds along a stone pathway from the entrance of the garden, he sees to the right a stairway leading from the Old Shoin. This was no doubt provided to make it possible to go directly from the Old Shoin to the Geppa-rō. A somewhat primitive grilled opening in the upper part of the outer wall of this passageway preserves a measure of continuity with the garden. Seen at the left in this photograph is the tip of the Moon-Viewing Platform.

34 The main house seen from the Middle Islands
Stepping stones lead from the Old Shoin down to the edge of the pond, from which one crosses two slatted arched bridges to reach the eastern Middle Island. At this point, one is directly in front of the Moon-Viewing Platform and can observe the full elegance of the roundish shingled roof of the Old Shoin balancing against its slightly upward-curving eaves. The echoing roofs of the Middle Shoin, Music Room, and New Palace recede to the left.

35 The east side of the Middle Shoin
In the Middle Shoin the eaves are 33.9 centimeters lower at the edge and the floor is 14.2 centimeters higher than in the Old Shoin (right). This section of the main house therefore appears to stand very high off the ground. That the overhang of the eaves is very short in comparison with other Japanese architecture of the same type is due to the placement of the shoji and rain shutters on the outer side of the veranda rather than the inner. Since this was not done until the latter half of the Edo period, the resulting "modern" look cannot be considered to have been part of the original design.

36–37 Stepping stones in the garden before the Middle Shoin
The stones seen here are part of a path leading across a stretch of moss in front of the Middle Shoin. Though the rocks appear to have been placed haphazardly, in fact much thought has been given to achieving a natural balance among their various irregularities. Furthermore, there is enough variation in height to create up-and-down movement as the visitor walks over them. Such subtle use of rocks is basic to traditional Japanese gardening. Particularly striking here is the fashion in which the arrangement in Plate 37 suggests the desultory flight of a butterfly.

38 The south side of the Old Shoin
Since the Middle Shoin, visible at left, was added on later, the original design of the Old Shoin can no longer be seen. As a result, the projection of the eaves seems too small in comparison with the rise of the gable. Another sort of imbalance arises from the contrast between the white base wall of the Old Shoin and the "freestanding" outer posts under the veranda of the Middle Shoin.

39–40 The main house seen from the south lawn

A lawn stretches out to the south of the Middle Shoin. When one looks across this flat area toward the gable of the Middle Shoin, the Old Shoin is visible in the distance on the right and the roof of the Music Room is in the left foreground. The long-legged Middle Shoin, with its white midriff and the somewhat festive latticework under its gable, looks refreshingly youthful in comparison with the solid, stable Old Shoin. Unfortunately, the linking between the Middle Shoin and the Music Room is rather clumsy, probably because of adjustments made when it became necessary to use the Music Room section as a connecting passageway to the New Palace.

Snow seems somehow to bring historical movements to a standstill (*Plate 40*). The violent shifts and changes in Prince Toshihito's career and the ardor of Prince Noritada's quest for knowledge are here crystallized into a black and white landscape.

41–42 Drainage gutter of the Middle Shoin

There are no roof gutters at the Katsura Palace, either on the main house or on the smaller buildings in the garden. One result is that much creative effort went into the arrangements made for draining off the rainwater that falls from the eaves. Since the Old Shoin is at the top of a small eminence, a row of medium size rocks is employed there to create two levels, at the lower of which there is a strip of gravel 48 centimeters wide that serves as a drainage ditch.

Beside the Middle Shoin, where the floor of the veranda is higher than in the Old Shoin and the posts underneath are exposed, two rows of brick-shaped stones are placed so that they project slightly above ground level, and the interval between them, which is 49 centimeters wide, is filled with gravel. Under the corner of the eaves on the southeast, there is a connecting rectangular drain 98 centimeters long and 88 centimeters wide, while along the south side there is a row of stepping stones parallel with the gutter. Beyond the stepping stones is a parallel row of tiles embedded in the ground and forming a clear demarcation between an inner

patch of moss and the outer lawn. The use of several straight lines with different textures reflects an aesthetic sense in harmony with twentieth-century tastes.

In the snow on a cloudy day in January (*Plate 42*), the contrasting textures in this arrangement are all the more prominent than in fair weather. While doubting that the designer actually foresaw this effect, one cannot help being impressed with the potential strength of the design that has evoked it. Here is a splendid example of "creating nature," which is so often the goal of traditional Japanese gardening techniques.

43–44 Stepping stones in front of the Music Room

The stepping stones leading past the south side of the Middle Shoin turn at the west corner and continue in front of the Music Room, but then come to an abrupt end. The reason is that there was once a court for football (*kemari*) in front of the New Palace and the path stopped at the edge of the court. The geometrical patterns seen here undergo subtle changes with the shifting of the seasons. In early summer (*Plate 44*), everything is fresh and green; in late fall (*Plate 43*) the hues are sober and subdued.

45 Zigzag line of the eaves of the Music Room and the New Palace

Under the zigzag line formed by the eaves, the aged look of the blackish brown posts and beams combines with the faint warm tints of the shoji to express the very essence of autumn. The shadows under the eaves already have the touch of forlornness that characterizes the season.

46 Shoji in the late fall

Since what is called the south side of the Middle Shoin faces not due south, but twenty-seven degrees toward the west, it receives more than its share of the evening sun. Seen here is the effect produced on the shoji by the slanting light of a rapidly sinking late autumn sun. Since the places where the strips of shoji paper are joined do not coincide with the frames underneath, the vertical lines at the seams add an irregular geometric pattern not unlike that of the surface of a stone castle embankment. Here is an excellent illustration of why shoji have become symbolic of Japanese architecture as a whole.

47 The east side of the New Palace

Like the Old Shoin and the Middle Shoin, the New Palace has a hipped-and-gabled shingle roof, seen here from across the lawn that once served as a *kemari* court. The lower hipped roof at right belongs to the Music Room. The intermediary position of the Music Room partly conceals the fact that in the New Palace the eaves are lower by 8.5 centimeters and the floor level by 38.8 centimeters than in the Middle Shoin, but the elevation of the New Palace is nevertheless obviously less lofty than the Middle Shoin. Indeed, the reduction in height combines with the rather large mass of the roof to make this section appear top-heavy. The total impression is one of solidity rather than lightness. The difference reflects a change in architectural fashions from the period of the Middle Shoin to that of the New Palace.

48 Detail of the west facade of the New Palace

The exterior of the New Palace is not the same as at the time of its construction, for the placement of rain shutters and shoji along the outer edge of the veranda was not carried out until after the middle of the Edo period. This is clear from a drawing of the Katsura Palace made around 1700 (*Figure 42*). In the original plans, only the railing ran along the outer periphery, and the shoji, along with wooden paneled doors that doubled as rain shutters, were placed along the inner rim, which is to say about six feet in from the outer posts. The veranda was therefore like the one on the south side of the Music Room. Although the present design differs from the original, the interplay of light between the shingled roof and the shoji is nevertheless beautiful. The changes in hue that accompany the shifting of the sunlight make it difficult to tell just what the

42. Detail of the "Complete Drawing of Prince Katsura's Country House," showing the main house, the Geppa-rō, and the Sumiyoshi Pine (*cf. Figure 17, page 113*).

natural colors of the materials are. *Sukiya*-style designers characteristically made the most of the natural tints and textures of the materials employed.

THE GEPPA-RŌ AND THE MIDDLE ISLANDS

Together with the main house, the area including the Geppa-rō and the two Middle Islands forms the nucleus of the house-and-garden complex. There is no doubt but that Prince Noritada, who was always seeking to recapture the romantic atmosphere of the *Tale of Genji*, consciously took as his model here the overall layout of the *shinden-zukuri* mansion of Heian times (*see Figure 24, page 123*), though the style of the buildings is different. If the Old Shoin is regarded as a counterpart to the central building of the *shinden* house, the general appearance of the area around the Middle Islands is very similar to the classic pattern, and the Geppa-rō corresponds closely to the "fishing pavilion" or "spring pavilion" of the Heian model. What is most remarkable is that the *shinden* style is not imitated, but grasped as an abstract spatial concept into which has been introduced the dramatic contrast between the somewhat conservative *shoin* style of the Old Shoin and the new *sukiya* style of the Geppa-rō. This is an example of the Manneristic approach, conditioned by a strong emphasis on intellectuality. It may well be that the insistently cerebral quality of the classicism seen here obscures the purely aesthetic value of this part of the Katsura garden. Nevertheless, the garden as a whole must be rated alongside that of the Shugaku-in Detached Palace as one of the greatest masterpieces of the tour-garden idiom.

49 The pond seen from the Geppa-rō

It is possible to go from a point just inside the Central Gate (*Plate 12*) directly up a climbing path of stepping stones to the Geppa-rō, but customarily the approach is made from the Old Shoin either by way of the Entrance Hall garden or from the exit with the grilled window at the northeast corner of the east veranda (*Plate 33*). The teahouse is at the top of an artificial hillock, about one meter above the ground level at the Old Shoin and high enough to require a stone retaining wall on the side adjacent to the pond. Thanks to this rise, this spot is the best in the garden from which to view the reflection of the moon in the water. The name Geppa-rō, "Moon-Wave Tower," is derived from a poem by Po Chü-i in which the moon is spoken of as a "jewel flickering in the heart of the waves." Between the teahouse and the pond are a number of larch trees (known in Japanese by a name that means "red pine"), whose reflection makes the image of the moon in the water seem all the more romantic.

50 The Geppa-rō seen from the Old Shoin

Though the ground on which the Geppa-rō stands is a little higher than the surrounding area, because of the numerous larches and plum trees growing around the teahouse, there are very few places from which it can be seen in full. That one of these is the Old Shoin is testimony to the close functional connection between the Geppa-rō and that building.

The Geppa-rō consists of a principal section, covered by a hipped shingle roof with a very slight bulge, and a small auxiliary section with a gabled roof on the south (front) side. This is exactly the type of casual, unassuming teahouse that one would expect to find near a residence like the Old Shoin. In front are a few plum trees, probably planted there to bear out an alternative name for the Geppa-rō, which is "Plum Teahouse."

51 The Geppa-rō seen from the Mount of Maples

The best place from which to view the Geppa-rō at a distance is along the shore adjacent to the Mount of Maples. At this point, most of the north side of the teahouse is visible (it can also be seen, though not as well, from the point of land on which the Sumiyoshi Pine stands). Since the roof on this side has a structurally meaningless gable, one supposes that the designer wanted to

emphasize its appearance from this angle, perhaps to call attention to its position beside the pond. Though the Geppa-rō is not classifiable as a "tower" (*rō*) by ordinary standards, it may have been called that because of its view out over the water, where the reflection of the moon can be seen. It might be noted in this connection that a twelfth-century text on gardening, *On Constructing Gardens* (*Sakutei-ki*), decrees that a "tower" is built for the purpose of viewing the moon.

Seen in the foreground here is the Sumiyoshi Pine.

52 Plaque in the Geppa-rō with a picture of a ship

This plaque hangs above the lintel between the dirt-floored section and the First Room of the Geppa-rō. The vessel depicted appears to be one of the "red-seal" ships that were engaged in government-licensed foreign trade during the late sixteenth and early seventeenth centuries, and the presence of the plaque here suggests that there was some connection between foreign trade and the building of the Geppa-rō. There is no firm historical evidence on this point, but it is a striking coincidence that the other plaque in the Geppa-rō—the one on the north side of the Middle Room—was inscribed by a Korean ambassador to Japan, who arrived in Kyoto in 1604. This plaque with the ship is said to have been hung in front of a shrine in Lower Katsura Village in 1605, before being brought to its present location.

53 The ceiling and ridge-support post in the Geppa-rō

Although the exterior of the Geppa-rō is quite ordinary, the interior reveals a number of unusual features. In the first place, instead of the normal roof-support framework seen in Japanese houses, we find a striking arrangement in which the main ridge-support is a bent, unbarked oak log rising from a beam that transects the building near the middle. Further support for the ridge is provided by slanting beams at the four corners. As noted in the text, the principle underlying this structure is the same as that of the balancing-man toy (*yajirōbei*). Reliance upon unorthodox

43. The decorated roof-underside of the dirt-floored section and First Room of the Geppa-rō seen from the Middle Room.

structures of this sort is another characteristic of *sukiya*-style architecture. Here, the felicitous result is a superb interior space.

54 Detail of the ceiling in the Geppa-rō

Shown in the color photograph is the upper part of the dirt-floored room in the Geppa-rō, seen from the Middle Room. The ceiling is of the type called *keshō-yaneura* (decorated roof-underside).

The beam across the middle of the teahouse, the upper door track hanging from it, and the frame of the shoji are all relatively thin and delicate. Consequently, what we notice is several sets of more or less vertical lines, all of which tend to draw our attention to the upper part of the space. The combination of elements is rhythmic, even poetic.

Figure 43 is a photograph of the Middle Room of the Geppa-rō taken from approximately the same point as in the plate. The plaque reads "Gekka," which means "Song of the Moon."

55 The Middle Islands

The view shown here is from the north side of the Geppa-rō. At present, there are two Middle Islands, western and eastern, but it appears that until the mid Edo period there was a third, farther to the east. No doubt the intention was to represent the Three Islands of the Immortals, Hōrai, Eishū, and Hōjō (called in Chinese P'eng-lai, Ying-chou, and Fang-chang), referred to in Japanese literature of the Heian period and springing ultimately from Taoist lore. The tiny pagoda made of stones (right center) is a finishing touch designed to emphasize the sacredness of the land where the immortals reside.

56 Amanohashidate seen from the Middle Islands

From the shore in front of the Old Shoin, a slatted bridge leads across a section of the pond to the first of the two Middle Islands, from which the visitor may view an arrangement representing Amanohashidate in miniature. One is thus standing in a Taoist paradise but looking across the water at a symbolic reproduction of

a real Japanese setting. This view is from the western island. It should be noted that formerly a bridge with red-lacquered railings, which crossed from the Maple Riding Lane to the promontory in front of the Shōkin-tei, was between the Middle Islands and Amanohashidate.

57 The Mount of Maples

The view is northward from the Geppa-rō. According to the *Record of the Country House at Katsura*, "the trees [on the Mount of Maples] were brought from Tatsuta, but there was one from Korea—leaves different, shallower lobes." Tatsuta refers to the area around the Tatsuta River (the lower part of the Ikoma River) in Yamato Province (Nara Prefecture), which was famous for its maples. This section of the garden is the earliest to take on the brilliant natural colors of fall. The "mountain" was created from a protective embankment that enclosed the first version of the Katsura Palace. It rises to a height of 12.8 meters above water level and is the highest point in the northern part of the garden.

58 Garden bridges seen from the inlet before the Shōi-ken

This photograph was taken from a boat near the mooring in front of the Shōi-ken (*Plates 88 and 89*). The bridge in the foreground connects (right to left) the Onrin-dō (*Plate 87*) with the lawn on the south side of the main house. The second bridge crosses from a point west of the Shōka-tei to the garden in front of the Old Shoin. Beyond these two earth-covered arches, the slatted bridge connects the eastern Middle Island with the western Middle Island. In the time of Prince Noritada, a fourth bridge—the one with red-lacquered railings mentioned in the caption to Plate 56—must also have been visible from this point. The line along which the bridges are placed runs from southwest to northeast and divides the pond into two almost equal parts. This must have been one of the most unusual and delightful vistas awaiting those who had the good fortune to view the garden by boat.

THE OUTER ARBOR AND
AMANOHASHIDATE

Japanese tour gardens are planned so that in walking through them, one always has the pond on one's right. In order to tour the Katsura Palace garden, the visitor retraces his steps through the Central Gate and back to a point about halfway along the Imperial Pathway. Just beyond the Mount of Maples, there is a break in the shrubbery on the right, which provides entry into the Maple Riding Lane—a long straight walk of forty-five meters paved with pebbles. About a quarter of the way down this, the garden path turns off to the left, and one walks across a series of stepping stones to the Outer Arbor (*soto-goshikake*). This entire eastern part of the garden may be considered the precinct of the Shōkin-tei. The approach to this teahouse is divided into two distinct stages. The first, called the Outer Pathway, continues to the end of the straight stone walk running in front of the Outer Arbor; the second, from here past the Drum Waterfall (*Plate 65*) and the Rocky Shore (*Plate 67*) to the stone bridge (*Plate 70*) in front of the Shōkin-tei Tearoom. Midway along this route is the Arbor for Four (*yotsu-goshikake*), also called the Manji-tei (*Figure 44*). In contrast to the area surrounding the Middle Islands, this part of the garden seems small in concept, but its design incorporates many of the more interesting techniques employed by Edo-period gardeners. The actual work of laying out this section was probably done in about 1647.

59 The Outer Arbor
At the point where the garden path branches off from the Maple Riding Lane, there was formerly a gate with a hedge fence on either side, but this has now disappeared. The Outer Arbor, to which the stepping stones lead, is a small open shelter that faces west and has a hipped roof thatched with miscanthus. On the right side of the arbor are benches for guests waiting to be taken to the Tearoom in

the Shōkin-tei; on the left side is an enclosed privy (*Plate 61*). By comparison with the impressive stone walk along the front of the arbor, the four oak logs that support the roof seem exceedingly thin and fragile. They impart a dreamlike quality—a sense of impermanence tinged with loneliness.

60 The ceiling of the Outer Arbor
Here is another example of the *keshō-yaneura* ceiling, similar in design and appearance to that of the Imperial Gate (*Plate 5*). The single heavy bamboo in the middle of the photograph represents a rafter. Attached to it is a lattice of smaller sticks of bamboo; reeds forming the underside of the miscanthus thatch have been placed over this frame. The thatch itself is visible at the outer edge (bottom). One marvels at the fashion in which designers working in the *sukiya* style employed the natural qualities of their materials to produce a decorative effect.

61 Detail of the wall outside the privy in the Outer Arbor
The privy on the north end of the Outer Arbor was not intended for actual use. It is purely ornamental, and its design is consequently stylistic, rather than functional. We can see from its presence here the determination of the *sukiya*-style designers to impose their creative stamp on even the smallest and most insignificant detail. Normally, a toilet would be hidden from the visitor's eye, but here it is employed as an *objet* of sorts. The stone seen in the color photograph is not only the foundation for the bamboo post standing on it, but also an integral part of the toilet fixture inside (*Figure 45*).

62 Water basin in front of the Outer Arbor
The arrangement shown here is at the north end of the walk in front of the Outer Arbor. A curving stone has been laid down for guests to stand on, and a square basin has been placed so that one of its corners fits into the elbow of the curve. The cavity for the water has two levels, a shallow upper square and a deeper inner

44. The Arbor for Four.

45. Interior of the privy in the Outer Arbor.

153

square set at a forty-five degree angle to the upper one. The small stone lantern at the left was placed here later to complete the arrangement, which is said to be in the style of Kobori Enshū.

63 Detail of the stone walk in front of the Outer Arbor

The straight stone-paved walk in front of the Outer Arbor is even more impressive than its counterpart in the garden before the Entrance Hall of the Old Shoin (*Plate 13*), for here the contrast in size of the component rocks is greater and their jagged edges have been left more in their natural state. Great finesse is to be seen in the placement of the pieces, but there is an overall tone of bravura, accented by the massive stepping stones adjacent to the walk. The design may be regarded as a boldly masculine one, balancing the femininity of the Outer Arbor itself.

64 Detail of Amanohashidate in the snow

The real Amanohashidate is a long sandbar stretching out into Miyatsu Bay in the Tango region (the northernmost part of Kyoto Prefecture). Since ancient times it has been counted as one of the three most magnificent sights in Japan. No doubt it had an additional special meaning for Prince Noritada, for it was adjacent to the village where his mother was born. In the Katsura garden, the two promontories that frame the sandbar are represented by two miniscule islands; the sandbar itself is portrayed by the long cut stone seen here. In the thin light of an early morning in winter, the snow-covered slab gives forth a soft glimmering light.

65 The Drum Waterfall

At the end of the stone walk shown in Plate 63, the path abruptly turns left, and one comes upon a modest stone bridge. This is the beginning of the Inner Pathway to the Tearoom in the Shōkin-tei. It is marked by a rock arrangement on the left representing the rapids and falls on the Ōi River, an upper part of the Katsura. The Ōi River flows through a deep gorge, celebrated for its beauty in the *Tales of Utsubo* and other classic writings. Since the tiny

waterfall in the highly abbreviated miniaturization at Katsura makes a sound something like that of a small Japanese drum, it is known as the Drum Waterfall. In the past, it would seem, the rhythmic tones could be heard in the Shōkin-tei. To a cultivated mind at leisure, the pleasant suggestion offered by this fabrication must have been more deeply impressive than the original landscape itself.

66 Amanohashidate and the Shōkin-tei seen from the Rocky Shore

After crossing the stone bridge in front of the Drum Waterfall, the visitor arrives at a reef where the stepping stones stand out slightly above the small rocks with which the shore is paved. As he emerges onto this "beach," the Shōkin-tei suddenly appears across the pond to his right, and a view of Amanohashidate in the foreground replaces the sequestered gorge and waterfall that he has just been contemplating. The shift from closed mountain ravine to open seashore is typical of the designer's search for the marvelous and beautiful—a touch of fancy that astonishes and delights the eye.

67 Stepping stones on the Rocky Shore

On the bank across from Amanohashidate, a shoreline is created with flattish, dark-gray pebbles embedded in the ground. The flatness is interrupted only by a line of stepping stones leading to the south. As one crosses here, the surrounding scenery is back-lighted, and one has the impression of being in a fantastic world without color.

68 Stone lantern at the tip of the Rocky Shore

On a tiny cape extending from the Rocky Shore is a small stone lantern, the light from which causes the stone bridge of Amano-hashidate to be reflected in the pond at night, creating another small world of fantasy. The lantern functions to establish a psychological link with the Shōkin-tei, thus relieving the feeling of solitude which the Outer Arbor engenders.

Toward the end of a long narrow pass beyond the Rocky Shore, there is a slight rise from which a two-pronged maple tree extends out over the pond. Near the roots of the tree is a stone lantern in Oribe style. Most of the column supporting the lantern is buried in the ground, but on the exposed topmost part, which is round, there are markings that appear to be an inscription of some sort. For about fifty years, roughly between 1920 and 1970, it was thought that the lantern was Christian in inspiration, and that the writing said PA, for *papa*, or PFS, for *pater et filius et spiritus sanctus* (*Figure 46*). In recent years, however, Kiichi Matsuda, an expert on European influence on Japan during the sixteenth and seventeenth centuries, has proved that there is no connection whatever with Christianity. Instead, he argues that the marks are related to the *kanoe saru* cult (*see below*). Because of the connection between the Shōkin-tei and the *kanoe saru* celebrations, Dr. Matsuda's theories seem all the more probable.

THE SHŌKIN-TEI

The Shōkin-tei is directly across the pond from the main house, to which it offers a fascinating contrast. The two buildings stand in a *yin-yang* relationship to each other. The main house, situated on high ground, basks in the cheerful light of the sun, but the Shōkin-tei, clinging close to the lower ground beside the pond, is in the shade much of the time. In style, the main house is an open, at least semiformal residence, while the Shōkin-tei resembles a closed, self-protective farmhouse.

The long, shady pathway from the Outer Arbor attempts to prevent the contrast between light and dark from becoming merely a visual pleasure and to convert it into an intellectual experience. Whereas the miniature view of the Ōi River and Amanohashidate reflect a mental approach to beauty, the Shōkin-tei has about it a sensual romanticism—spirited but at the same time cool and soundless.

The name of the Shōkin-tei, which means "Pine-Lute Pavilion," was taken from a poem by Itsuki-no-miya Nyōgo about the mingling of the sound of the lute with the soughing of the wind through pine trees in the mountains. It is significant that the poem was composed on the night of the cyclical day *kanoe saru*, "metal and the monkey," for this was a day that had special meaning to the Japanese of the past. From early times, it had been said that those who slept on this night would not only have a run of very bad luck but also have their lives shortened. Moreover, if a woman conceived on the night of the day in question, the child she bore would grow up to be either a weakling or a thief. People were enjoined to remain awake on this night to avoid bringing bad fortune upon themselves. Chinese (Taoist) superstitions about *kanoe saru*, which first entered Japan in the Heian period, were widespread by the seventeenth century. It was a common practice in both Japan and China to hold an all-night drinking party each time the day occurred, and the Shōkin-tei was employed as the setting for such celebrations. It is accordingly "night-oriented." By the same token, the section of the garden lying before its First and Second Rooms was considered to be the "Face of Night." The metaphor was apt, since the area was so designed that it darkened earlier than other parts of the garden.

69 The northeast side of the Shōkin-tei
The visitor does not come face to face with the Shōkin-tei until he arrives at the end of the Inner Pathway, just before the stone bridge that crosses to the Tearoom. On the surface at least, the original Shōkin-tei might be described as an ordinary teahouse with a hipped-and-gabled thatch roof (*Plate 66*), but the addition to its reticent form of expression of the Tearoom and back section with its shingled roof and the pantry with its tiled roof (*Plate 82*) somehow makes the building seem strange and fantastic.

70 Stone bridge at the Shōkin-tei
To reach the Shōkin-tei, it is necessary to cross this massive granite

46. Oribe-style lantern near the Shōkin-tei, formerly called the Kirishitan-dōrō ("Christian Lantern").

slab, which is 5.9 meters long, 70 centimeters wide, and 36 centimeters thick. The left side of the slab, which is seen from downstream, is in the form in which it was cut at the quarry, but the surface of the right side has been straightened by a hammer or a chisel. The top surface has been roughened in the central section to provide surer footing.

71 Front wall of the Shōkin-tei Tearoom

Having crossed the stone bridge, one stands before the Tearoom of the Shōkin-tei. On the right side of the bridge is a place where guests for the tea ceremony could wash their hands in the flowing water of the pond (*Plate* 73) before approaching the front of the Tearoom, which is seen here.

The door to the Tearoom is marked by the square wooden panel on the right side of the middle level. Since it is only half as high as a normal door, visitors had to enter on their knees. Running three-quarters of the way across the wall is a long window covered by a bamboo grille, above and to the left of which are smaller windows of the type known as *shitajimado* (a window that consists merely of a hole in the wall, with the lathing left exposed; in fact, what appears to be the lathing is often an ornamental grille attached within the wall to the real lathing). The grouping of the three windows seen here is thought to be in the style of Kobori Enshū.

It appears that the thatched section of the Shōkin-tei (the First and Second Rooms) was built first and the Tearoom added on by Prince Noritada sometime around 1647. This addition was presumably made to introduce new styles that had come into fashion since the construction of the original building.

72 Interior of the Shōkin-tei Tearoom

The Tearoom proper is a three-mat room with a small extension called a *daime*. When the visitor enters the low door, he sees straight ahead the arrangement shown here. He will also see to his immediate left the tokonoma and beside that the entrance for the person serving tea. At bottom left in the photograph is the hearth,

covered by lacquered boards. Behind this on the right is a curving log which acts as the terminus of a small projecting wall running from midway up the post to the ceiling. At far back are three *shitajimado* covered with shoji. All of these features are typical of teahouse architecture, which aimed at making the tearoom a microcosm to itself.

73 Rock arrangement in the pond beside the Shōkin-tei Tearoom

This arrangement of three large stones set in the pond was intended as a place where guests invited for the tea ceremony could wash their hands in running water. The idea, which is said to have come from Kobori Enshū, was no doubt both novel and appealing to guests accustomed to using the inert water of ordinary stone basins.

74 Water basin before the First Room of the Shōkin-tei

From the front of the Tearoom, the path leads around to the west side of the Shōkin-tei. There, on the shore in front of the First Room, is a water basin consisting merely of a rock with a cavity chiseled out of its top. As the visitor stands on the rock in front of the basin, he sees in the water a series of overlapping images formed by rock arrangements placed in the pond itself—a translucent image somehow different from that experienced at the "running-water basin" in Plate 73.

75 Amanohashidate backed by the "Face of Night"

When the Shōkin-tei was used for night gatherings such as those connected with the day of metal and the monkey, the guests sat in the First and Second Rooms, which formed the body of the section under the thatched roof, and looked out at the "Face of Night," an area which darkened early because of the thick growth of plants. The sunlight remained longest on the curving stone bridge of Amanohashidate, causing it to appear to subside gradually into the blackness around it. The effect was one of mysterious, otherworldly tranquillity. On evenings when the "Face of Night" was illumined by the reflection of the moon, the gradual transformation must have seemed even more ethereal.

76 The west side of the Shōkin-tei

Here the Shōkin-tei is seen across the pond from the Geppa-rō early on a spring day. Since it is the rainy season, the scene is veiled in a light mist, which suggests a valley deep in the mountains. The large cryptomeria tree leaning out over the water to the right may well have been planted here when the palace was first built. Formerly, the bridge with red-lacquered railings, mentioned elsewhere, ran from a point near the foot of the tree directly across the pond to the end of the Maple Riding Lane, no doubt adding an element of grace and color reminiscent of Heian-period styles. It is conjectured that when the present Tearoom was added to the Shōkin-tei, a new approach—the one used today—was built around the north shore of the pond. Presumably the older bridge was removed at this time.

77 Outdoor pantry under the eaves of the Shōkin-tei

On the northwest side of the Shōkin-tei, the overhang of the eaves is nearly two meters. Much of the unfloored loggia (*tsuchibisashi*) underneath is taken up by an outdoor pantry (*mizuya*) with an earthen oven. This section has a *keshō-yaneura* ceiling of the sort seen in the Geppa-rō and the Outer Arbor. The supporting columns are oak logs, left in their natural state, which contribute greatly to the general air of rusticity. The hearth, the small set of shelves beside it, and the low bamboo wall backing the shelves are in the style of Kobori Enshū. This pantry was probably installed for the purpose of making steeped tea (as distinguished from ceremonial tea, made by pouring hot water over powdered tea leaves and stirring rapidly with a whisk), which appears to have been popular when the Shōkin-tei was built. The "pavement" of pebbles in the loggia brings to mind the pebbled ground of the shore on the opposite side of the pond and thus acts as a psychological link

between the Shōkin-tei and the "Face of Night" of which the shore forms a part.

78 Amanohashidate seen from the Second Room of the Shōkin-tei

On each of the two outer sides of the Second Room in the Shōkin-tei there are two pairs of wooden doors with vertical frames and one pair of shoji. In addition, on the northwest side there is a transom window, in a slightly deformed elliptical shape, with shoji that slide out of sight. As in the Second Room of the main building, there is neither a *nageshi* beneath the transom nor a strut at the center. From here, one looks out through the loggia and across an expanse of lawn toward Amanohashidate, which is part of the "Face of Night." Since the Shōkin-tei is in the shade much of the time, the view it commands tends to look particularly sunny and bright, but on a moonlit night the same scene becomes a soft, faintly glowing vision from a different world.

79 Tokonoma and cabinets in the First Room of the Shōkin-tei

The First and Second Rooms make up the main body of the Shōkin-tei, and together with the outdoor pantry in the northwest loggia (*Plate 77*) they probably constituted the whole of Prince Noritada's concept at the time when the building was constructed. Combined, the First and Second Rooms form an L-shaped parlor with an area of seventeen mats. The posts are cryptomeria logs, planed so that the bark is left only on the four corners. The roof is of cryptomeria boards with a curving grain. As in the main house and the Geppa-rō, the wood has been stained and the walls have the natural ochre finish of the clay from which they are made. A colorful, yet at the same time cool, effect is produced by the blue-and-white checkered paper on the walls of the tokonoma and the sliding panels between the First Room and the Second Room. As noted in the text, this paper was produced in Kaga Province, the birthplace of Prince Noritada's wife, and was probably designed around the time of the prince's marriage.

Two built-in cabinets are next to the tokonoma. The upper one has door leaves of cryptomeria, opening outward; the lower one has sliding paper-covered panels decorated, as are the panels in the First Room of the Middle Shoin, with ink paintings by Kanō Tan'yū.

80 Detail showing the hearth and upper cabinets in the First Room of the Shōkin-tei

The hearth and cabinets shown here are around a corner to the right of the tokonoma seen in Plate 79. The hearth, which is of stone, was used for heating when Prince Noritada and his friends gathered here to view the moon on wintry nights. The paintings on the cabinet doors, which depict small birds playing on a shore, are by Kanō Tan'yū, and the metal handles in the form of tied cords are said to have been made by Kachō, to whom the door handles in the Middle Shoin are also attributed.

81 The Middle Islands seen from the First Room of the Shōkin-tei

The outer sides of the First Room of the Shōkin-tei are fitted only with shoji, rather than with a combination of shoji and wooden doors as in the Second Room. The reason is that the roof overhangs so far that wooden doors were considered unnecessary. The bottom quarters of the shoji, however, have wooden panels that protect the interior against water splashing from the ground. The transom on the west, which has a rough and perfunctory bamboo grille, provides a view of the underside of the eaves and the tops of the unbarked oak posts, which otherwise appear from the interior to be growing trees. In the use of natural logs of this sort, we see another instance in which the *sukiya*-style builder sought to "create nature." At the edge of the lawn on this side, across from the eastern Middle Island, is the boat mooring, toward which the arrow-shaped rock rising from among the pebbles under the eaves seems to be pointing the way. Another eccentric touch is the slight list ot the stone lantern.

82 The Shōkin-tei seen from the southwest

This is a backward look from the path leading from the Shōkin-tei to the Shōka-tei. It can be clearly seen from this photograph that the L-shaped hipped-and-gabled thatch roof on the left, which covers the First and Second Rooms, is an entity unto itself, and it is virtually certain that the original Shōkin-tei consisted of this section only. The extension on the right with the reddish earthen walls and a tiled pent roof is a pantry, added on after the Tearoom on the northeast side was built. The strip of cut stones along the edge of the pond is the boat mooring. The water here is very still, and the reflection of the Shōkin-tei appears as a phantom space below the surface of the pond.

THE SHŌKA-TEI, THE ONRIN-DŌ, AND THE SHŌI-KEN

Shortly after leaving the Shōkin-tei, the visitor reaches a point near the eastern extremity of the garden where the distance from the main house is greater than anywhere else along the garden path. From here on, the sights along the way come with less frequency than in the northeast section, and the walk seems more leisurely. Instead of feeling that one is being ushered past a concentration of visual delights, one gradually relaxes and takes in the scenery as it presents itself.

This part of the garden is centered upon an island called Ōyamashima ("Great Mountain Island"), which is linked with the "mainland" by three arching dirt-covered bridges. One of these is the approach from the Shōkin-tei on the east; another crosses southward to the Shōi-ken; the third extends northward to the main house. Whereas the mean level of the ground in the Katsura Palace compound is 23 meters above sea level, Ōyamashima rises to a height of 28 meters. The Shōka-tei is situated at the top, with the Onrin-dō at the foot of the mountain on the west side.

The Onrin-dō is a sort of family shrine, where the cenotaphs of members of the house of Hachijō are enshrined, along with a portrait of and letters written by Hosokawa Yūsai, whom Prince Noritada regarded as his mentor in matters of scholarship. The little temple may be regarded as signifying that Katsura was the prince's spiritual home. Though the other buildings in the garden are in the *sukiya* style, the Onrin-dō alone follows the lines of Buddhist architecture, with an emphasis on Chinese elements.

Across the pond from the Onrin-dō, at the western end of the garden, stands the Shōi-ken, which was Prince Noritada's private study. In general, this section of the garden was designed to be a broad and cheerful setting for the prince's intellectual activities, an area where he could give free vent to his thoughts and reveries. In another sense, it is a "debriefing" area where one can collect oneself before taking leave of Katsura's land of fantasy.

83 Bamboo grove in the Valley of Fireflies
To the left of the crossing from the Shōkin-tei to Ōyamashima is a deep inlet known as the Valley of Fireflies. The thick growth of bamboo suggests a sequestered ravine, where in the summer the air might from time to time be streaked with the languid light of fireflies.

84 The north side of the Shōka-tei
After passing the Valley of Fireflies, the visitor arrives in a "forest" of cryptomeria trees, where a climbing path of stepping stones leads to the Shōka-tei. Though the height of the rise is only five meters, the path is so steep that it is difficult to see the top from the bottom. Near the summit, the sky comes into view again, and one finds oneself before the extremely simple and bucolic teahouse. To strengthen the impression that this is a teashop of the sort often found at mountain passes, a shop curtain (*noren*) is hung across the front, its individual widths of cloth as likely as not waving gently in the breeze. It is said that Prince Noritada had this teahouse moved here from his residence in Imadegawa in about 1647.

85 Interior of the Shōka-tei seen from the west side
The name of the teahouse means "Flower-Appreciation Pavilion," and it was intended as a bower from which guests could admire the abundant cherry blossoms that bloom in this vicinity in the spring. The interior is therefore a spectator gallery of sorts, with tatami on three sides and an unfloored area with a clay stove in the center. The front opening is 3.94 meters wide, and the interior depth only 2.97 meters. In keeping with the function, the only posts on the front are the two unbarked oak logs needed at the corners to support the roof. There is thus an uninterrupted view, the openness of which is accented by windows (*shitajimado*) in the clay walls. The whole design of the teahouse may be regarded as an intellectual formalization of the "humble abode" as it is referred to in certain polite, self-deprecating Japanese phrases.

86 Path leading down from the Shōka-tei to the Onrin-dō
From the Shōka-tei, one can see, though the trees, the whole of the main house—a cheerful panorama that one could hardly have imagined from the ground-hugging Shōkin-tei. As one descends the path shown here to the Onrin-dō, one experiences a naturally accelerating rhythm, yet the memory of the height of the Shōka-tei seems to pull at one from behind.

87 Stepping stones in front of the Onrin-dō
The bulging tile roof of the Onrin-dō gives it a somewhat exotic look, emphasized by the curving gable (*karahafu*) over the entranceway (*Figure 47*). On the north side of the little temple, the natural stepping stones seen in Plate 86 suddenly give way to the squarecut granite stones shown here, which cross in desultory fashion over the pebbled rain gutter. The design is one of superb nonchalance—one might say immaculate carelessness. At top center in the photograph is the shaft of a stone lantern, on the hexagonal base of which has been carved a twelve-petal lotus blossom. This adds a Buddhist touch, which reminds us that the Onrin-dō is a memorial to the dead.

47. The Onrin-dō seen from the lawn in front of the main house

48. The unfloored loggia of the Shōi-ken. In the upper middle of the picture is the plaque on which the name of the building is written; beneath that are the six round windows.

88 The north side of the Shōi-ken

From the Onrin-dō an earth-covered bridge crosses to the lawn in front of the New Palace. The path, which continues along the southern edge of the grass and is paved with pebbles, is called the Plum Riding Lane because it is lined on both sides with plum trees. South of this is a squared, deliberately artificial inlet of the pond, beyond which stands the Shōi-ken. The main roof of this building, which is hipped, is covered with thatch, but the auxiliary eaves on the north and east sides are shingled, in a fashion widely employed for the houses of fishermen. Stone steps along the southern edge of the inlet form a boat mooring. Embarking here and rowing from the inlet, one comes upon the view shown in Plate 58.

89 Three Lights Lantern at the Shōi-ken

This diminutive lantern, which throws light on the boat mooring before the Shōi-ken, has neither shaft nor pedestal, and its rounded lid lacks the customary overhang. Since it has openings on its back and front sides which represent the sun, a crescent moon, and stars, it is known as the "Three Lights Lantern." In keeping with the somewhat cynical tone of the Shōi-ken, it appears to be taking a down-to-earth, frog's-eye view of the world about it.

90 Plaque and windows under the front eaves of the Shōi-ken

The name Shōi-ken, which means "Laughing-Thoughts Pavilion," is said to have been inspired by a passage in a poem by Li Po:

> When they ask me what I think
> Of living in the azure mountains,
> I laugh and do not answer
> That my heart here finds rest—
> The peach blossoms and the flowing stream
> Go far, far away.
> There is another universe
> Where there are no men.

For Prince Noritada, who immersed himself in his studies of Japanese and Chinese literature, the Shōi-ken was the haven where he could best put away outside cares and pursue his own thoughts—a free and secluded paradise where he confronted not other men and women, but the great universe.

Above the entrance, on the north side of the Entry Room, there is an unusual row of six round windows (shitajimado), which appear to symbolize Li Po's laughing at the world. These have been described as "windows of the four seasons," but for reasons that are unclear. A more probable explanation is that they represent six elements from which the universe was considered by some Chinese thinkers to be composed: yin and yang, wind and rain, darkness and light. In any case, the prominence with which they are displayed suggests that they are intended as a sardonic comment on the conventions of ordinary minds. As such, they can be seen as an expression of the Manneristic view of aesthetics.

The plaque on which the name of the building is inscribed was written by Prince Noritada's uncle, the Priestly Imperial Prince Ryōjo (Figure 48).

91 The Middle Room of the Shōi-ken

From the entrance of the Shōi-ken, one looks directly across the anteroom with the six round windows to the Middle Room, on the south side of which is a three-quarters-length picture window. This opening is called, appropriately enough, an "elbow-rest window" (hijikake-mado), for the sill is just high enough to prop one's elbow on when seated beside it. A good view being a requisite for this type of window, the original design called for a row of spirea outside, beyond which the fields of Lower Katsura Village could be seen.

On the low wall panel below the window, a band of gold foil runs diagonally from the upper left to the lower right. Cut to fit into the trianglar space left at the corners are pieces of velvet with a four-color checkered pattern. This overall design is most unusual, not only because the cloth was imported, but also because this sort of stark diagonal composition is virtually unknown in Japanese tradition. One has the impression of a bright ray of sun streaking through the clouds.

92 Cabinets in the Third Room of the Shōi-ken

On the east side of the Middle Room (also called the Second Room) of the Shōi-ken is the First Room, which has a *shoin* window, and on the west side is the Third Room, where there are a pantry on the north side and the cabinets shown here on the west side. In addition to these rooms, the building also has a fairly spacious kitchen at the west end and a large closet, as well as a toilet, at the east end. The Shōi-ken is thus a complete small house, where Prince Noritada might reside in comfort for some length of time, if he so wished.

The Third Room, which is next to the kitchen, was probably a dining room, and the cabinets in the photograph may well have been used for dishes and the like. The design on the door panels is abstract, but may have been intended to represent a sea of clouds in the sky.

93 Pantry in the Third Room of the Shōi-ken

The architectural details of the Shōi-ken are in the same general idiom as those of the Shōkin-tei: cryptomeria posts planed so that the bark is left on the corners; no *nageshi*; ceiling panels of cryptomeria board with curving grain; a combination of earthen walls in places and striking wall coverings in others. The presence of the little pantry shown here on the north side of the Third Room makes it clear that the Shōi-ken was intended to be more private than the Shōkin-tei.

Visible through the sketchy grille of the pantry window is the lawn in front of the New Palace.

94 Detail of the thatched roof of the Shōi-ken

The thatched roof of the Shōi-ken is especially plain in appearance, because, unlike the roofs of the Shōkin-tei and the Shōka-tei, it is not interrupted by gables. The roof line has a roundish bulge, and the whole superstructure hovers over the ground like a hen protecting her brood. At the ends of the ridge, bamboo projections patterned on those used in farmhouses as snowbreakers shoot forcefully outward as symbols of a creative spirit determined to persevere through the long snow of winter.

DRAWINGS OF THE KATSURA PALACE

The measurements given in the architectural drawings are in *shaku*, a traditional Japanese unit of length almost exactly equivalent to an English foot, or 30.3 centimeters. For conversion of *shaku* to the metric system, see the scale accompanying each drawing.

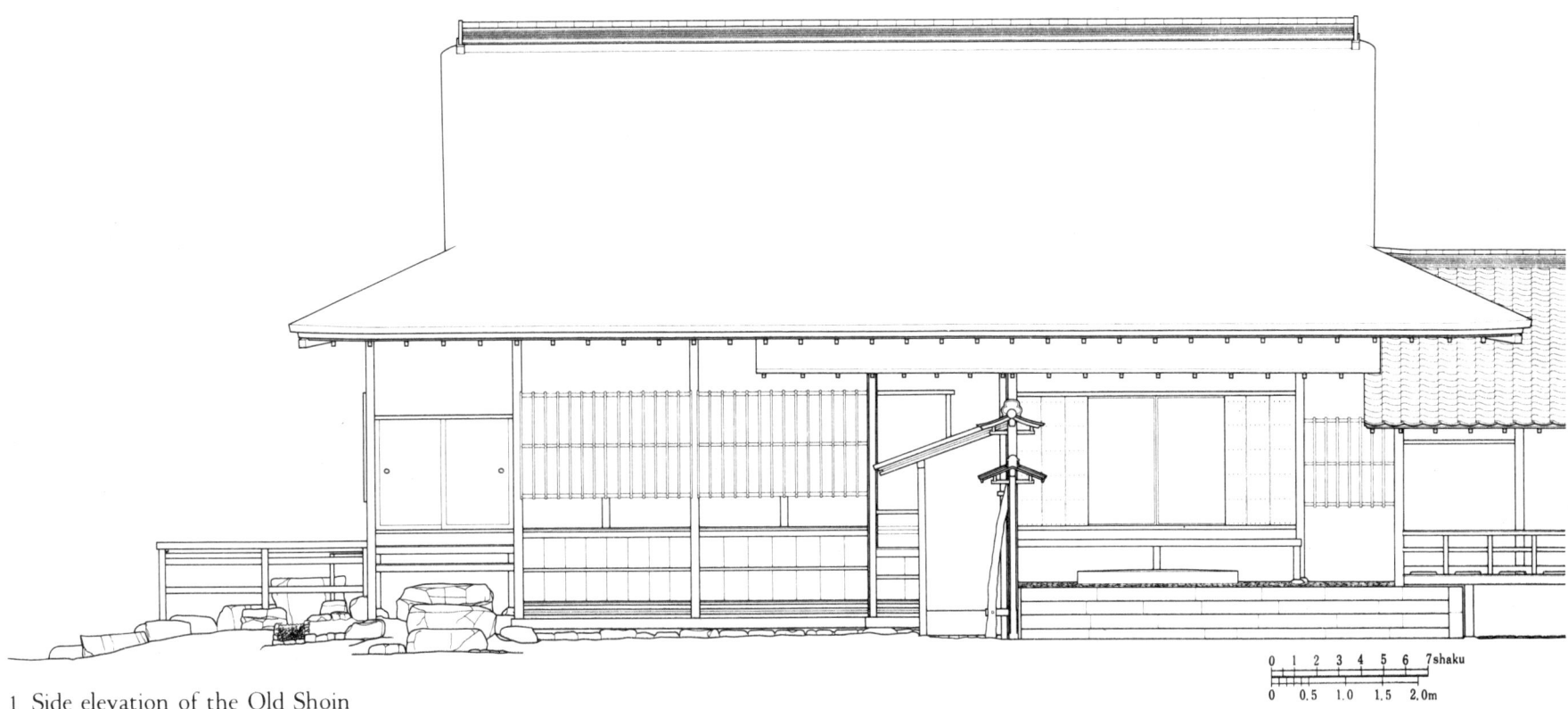

1 Side elevation of the Old Shoin

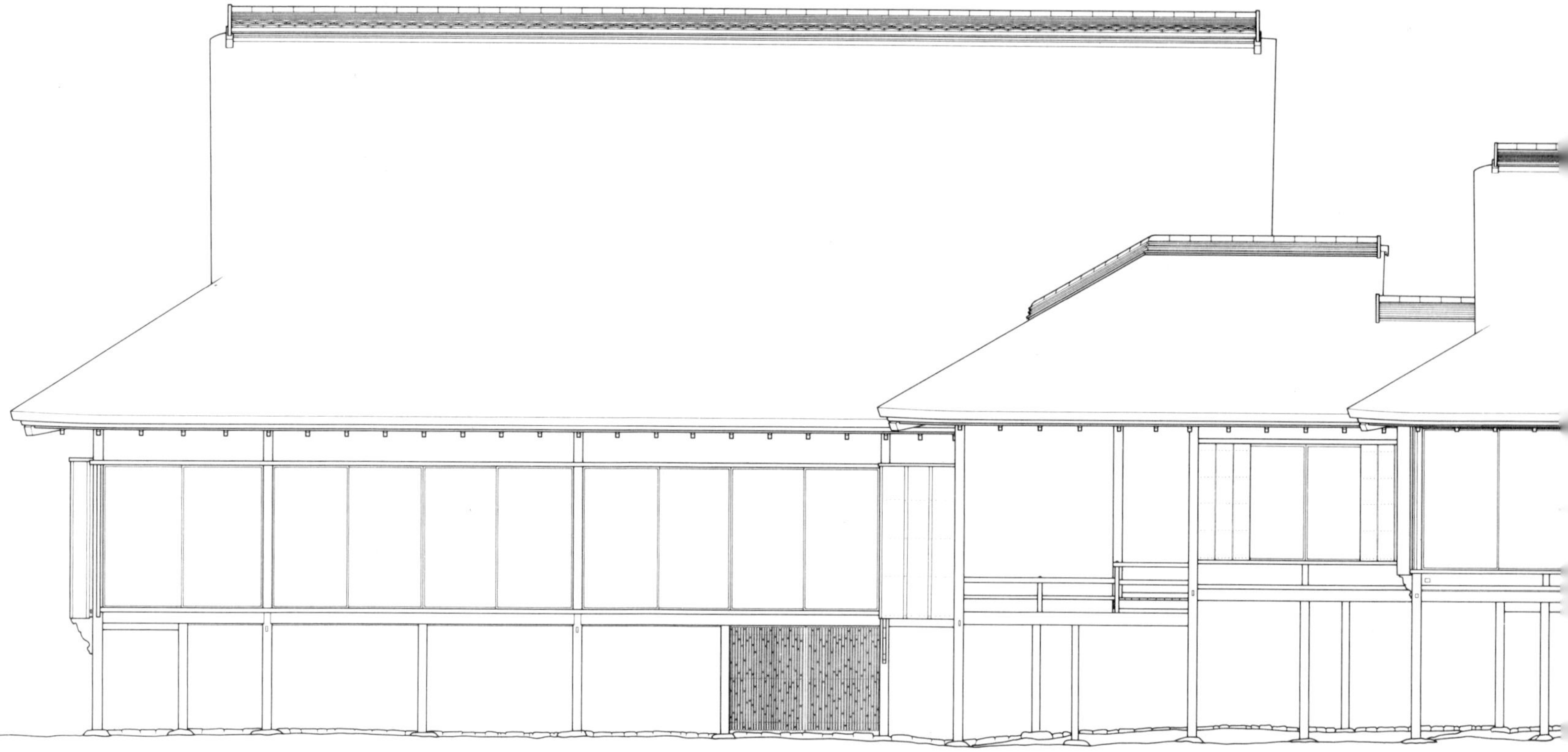

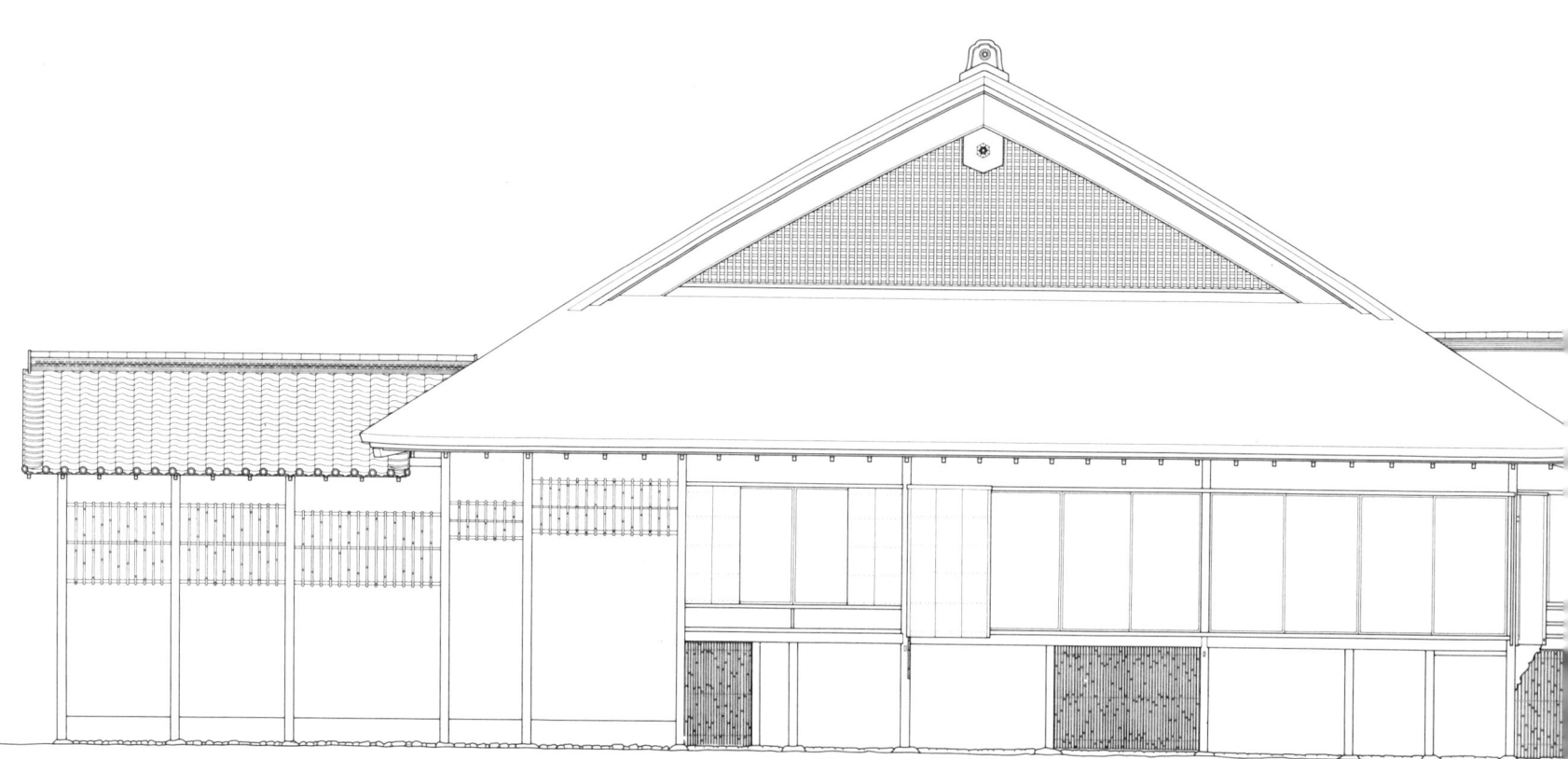

2 Front elevation of the main building

3 Side elevation of the main building

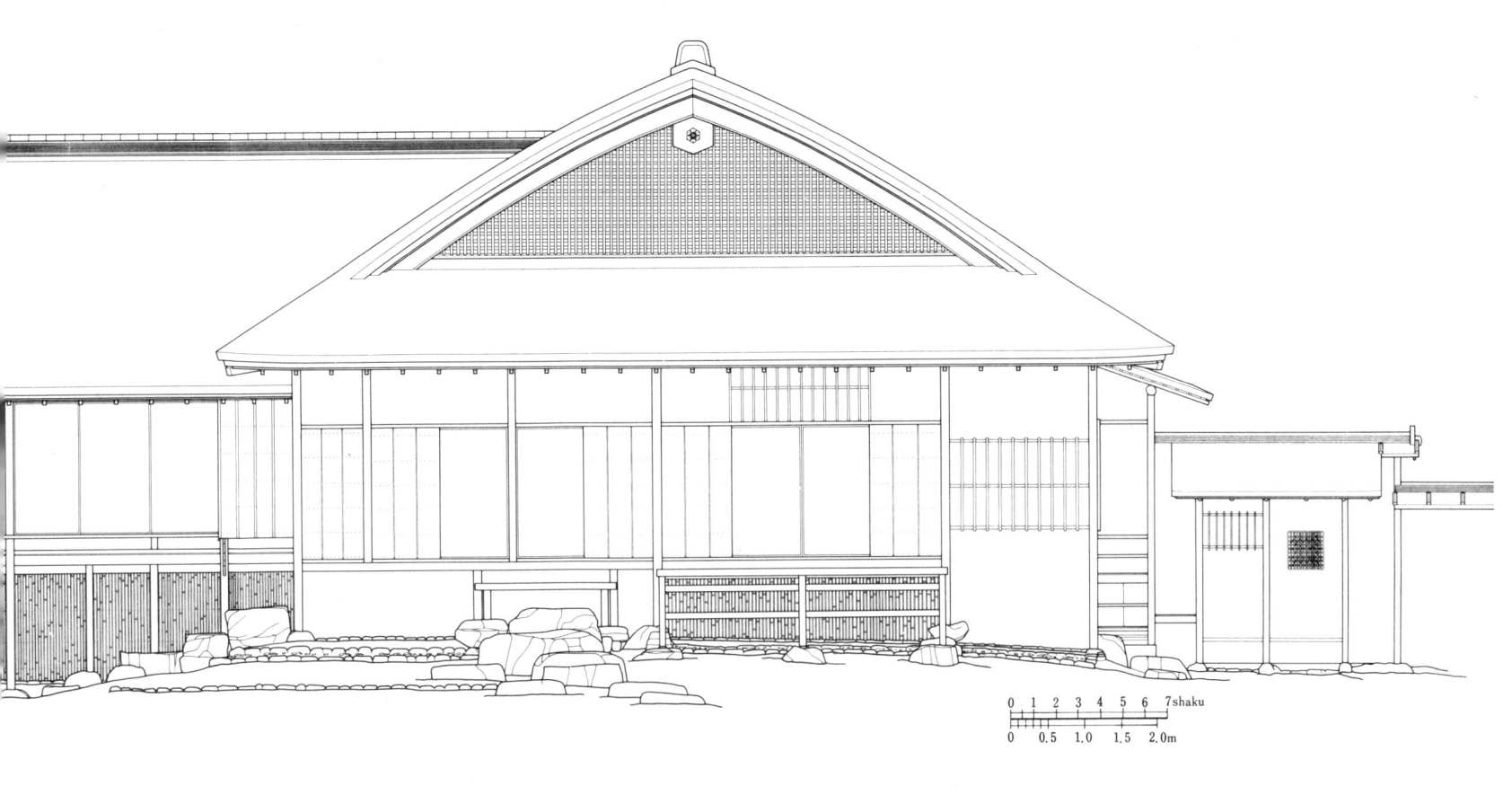

0 1 2 3 4 5 6 7shaku
0 0.5 1.0 1.5 2.0m

0 1 2 3 4 5 6 7shaku
0 0.5 1.0 1.5 2.0m

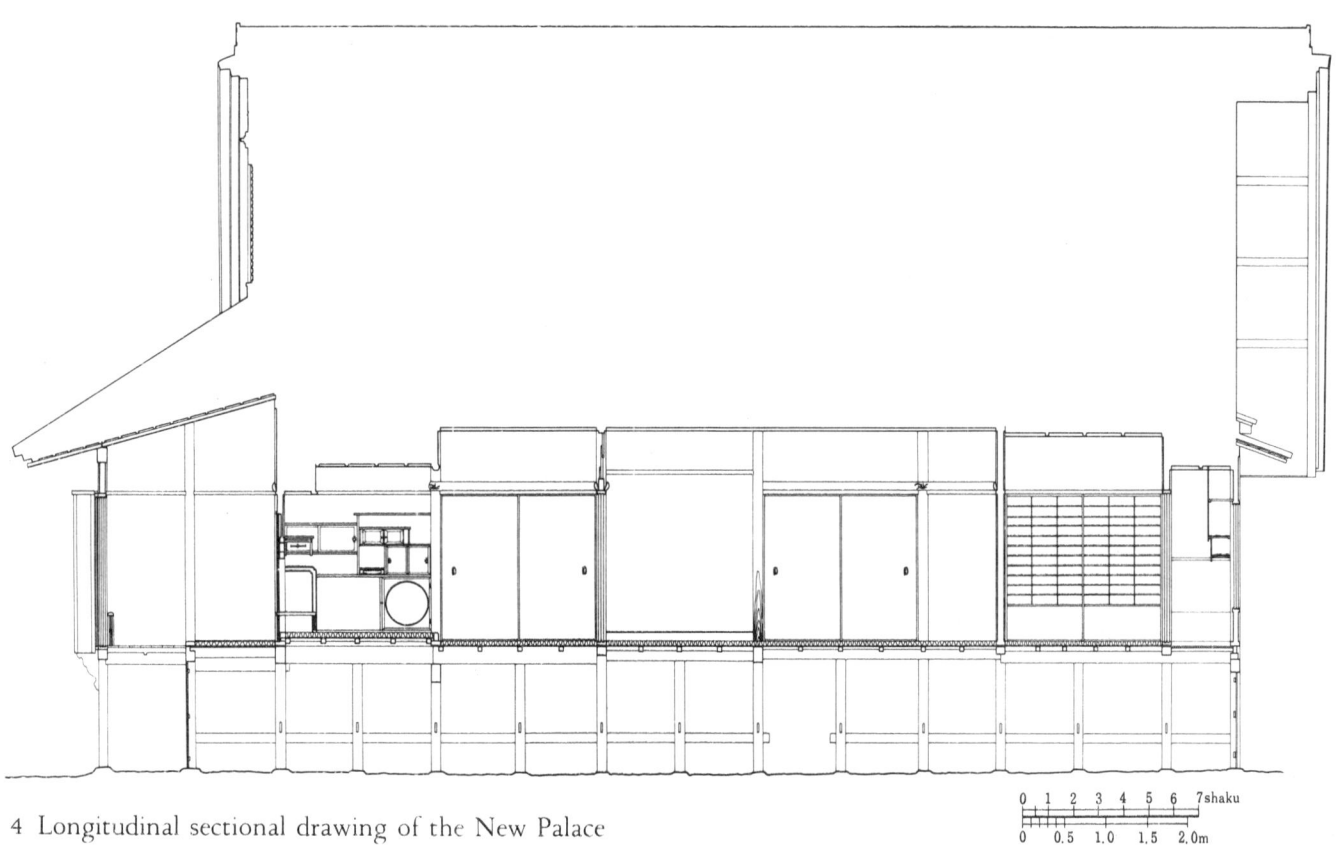

4 Longitudinal sectional drawing of the New Palace

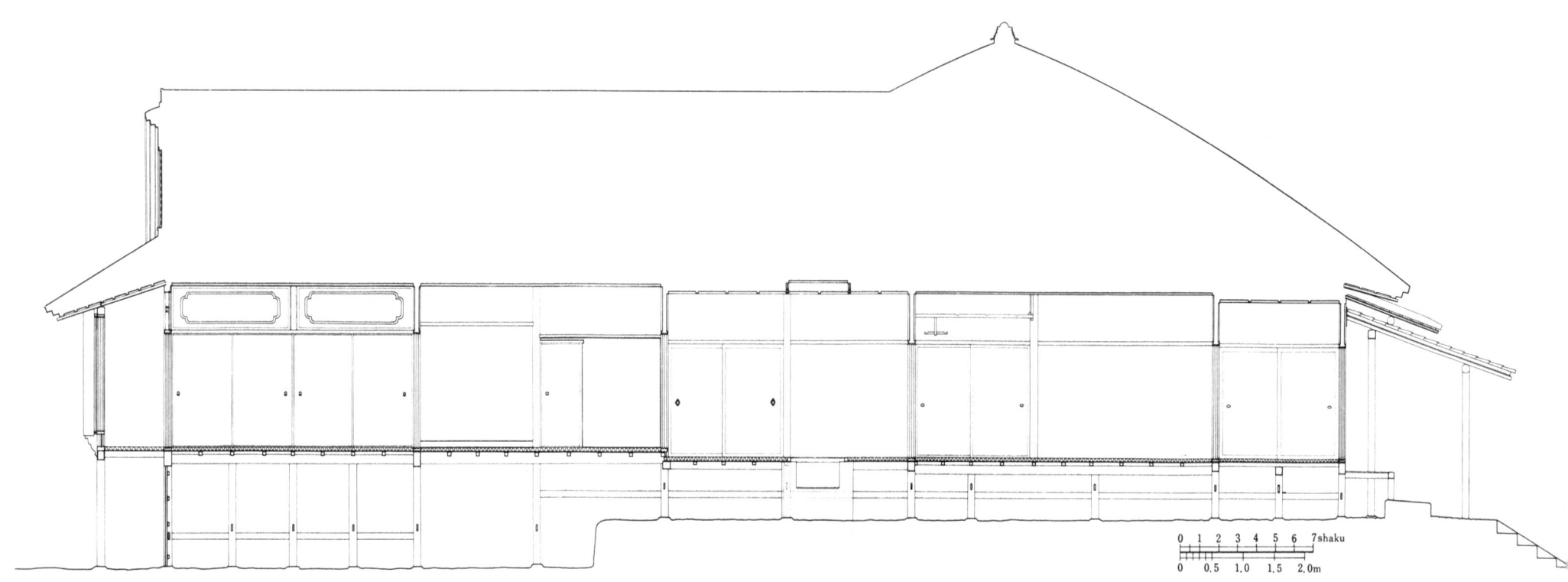

5 Longitudinal sectional drawing of the Middle Shoin and Old Shoin

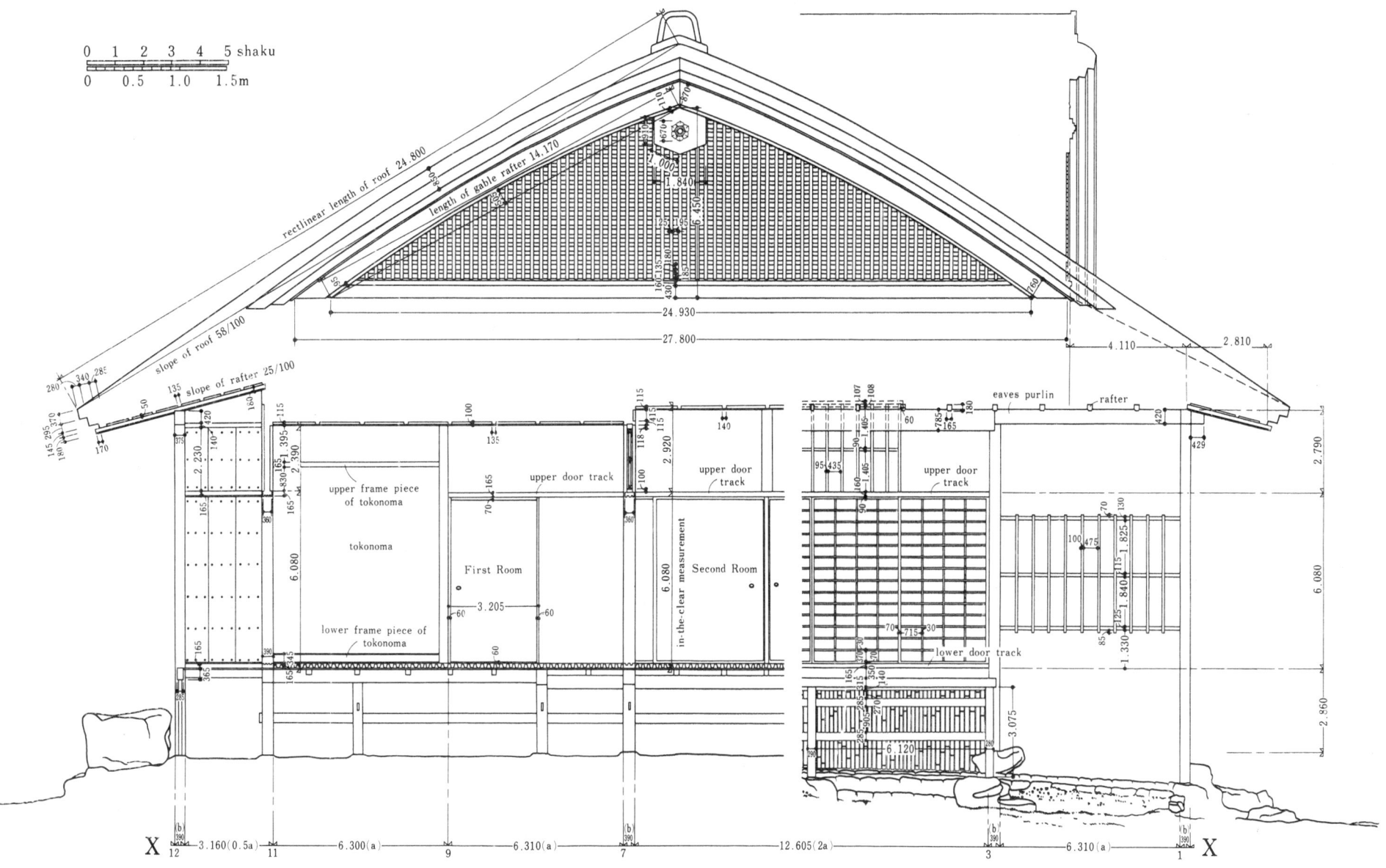

0 1 2 3 4 5 shaku
0   0.5   1.0   1.5m

rectilinear length of roof 24.800
length of gable rafter 14.170

slope of roof 58/100
slope of rafter 25/100

24.930
27.800

4.110
2.810

eaves purlin
rafter

2.790

upper frame piece of tokonoma

tokonoma

upper door track

upper door track

upper door track

First Room

Second Room

in-the-clear measurement

6.080

6.080

6.080

lower frame piece of tokonoma

lower door track

3.205

2.860

3.075

3.160(0.5a)
6.300(a)
6.310(a)
12.605(2a)
6.310(a)

X 12   11   9   7   3   1 X

6 Longitudinal sectional drawing of the Old Shoin

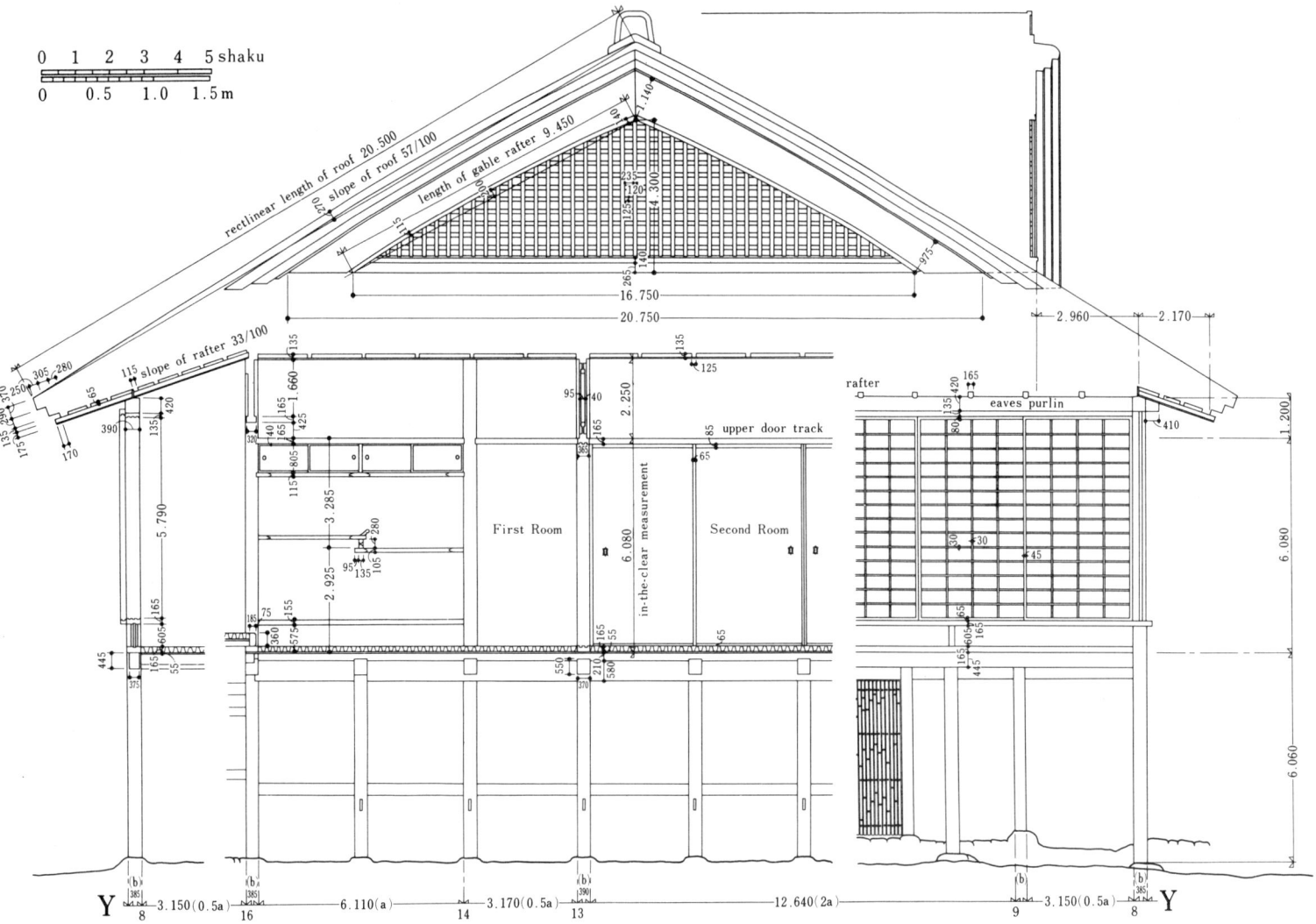

0 1 2 3 4 5 shaku
0 0.5 1.0 1.5 m

rectilinear length of roof 20.500
slope of roof 57/100
length of gable rafter 9.450

16.750
20.750
2.960
2.170

slope of rafter 33/100

First Room
Second Room

in-the-clear measurement 6.080

upper door track

rafter
eaves purlin

1.660
3.285
2.925
5.790

6.110(a)
3.150(0.5a)
3.170(0.5a)
12.640(2a)
3.150(0.5a)

Y
8
16
14
13
9
8
Y

7 Transverse sectional drawing of the Middle Shoin

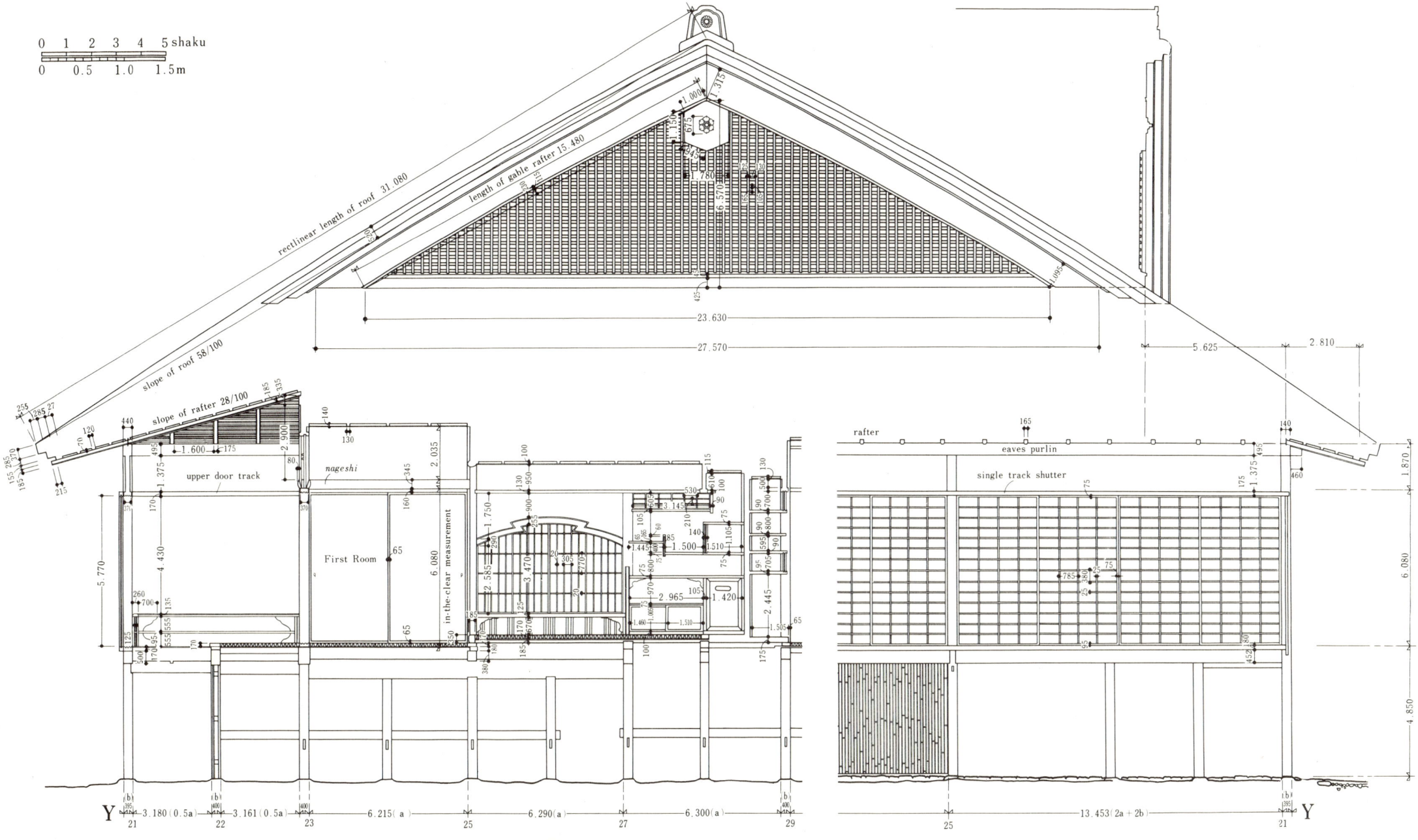

0 1 2 3 4 5 shaku
0 0.5 1.0 1.5 m

rectilinear length of roof 31.080
length of gable rafter 15.480
slope of roof 58/100
slope of rafter 28/100

23.630
27.570
5.625
2.810

upper door track
nageshi
First Room
in-the-clear measurement

rafter
eaves purlin
single track shutter

6.080

4.850

Y
21   22   23   25   27   29
3.180(0.5a) 3.161(0.5a) 6.215(a) 6.290(a) 6.300(a)

25   21
13.453(2a+2b)   Y

8 Transverse sectional drawing of the New Palace

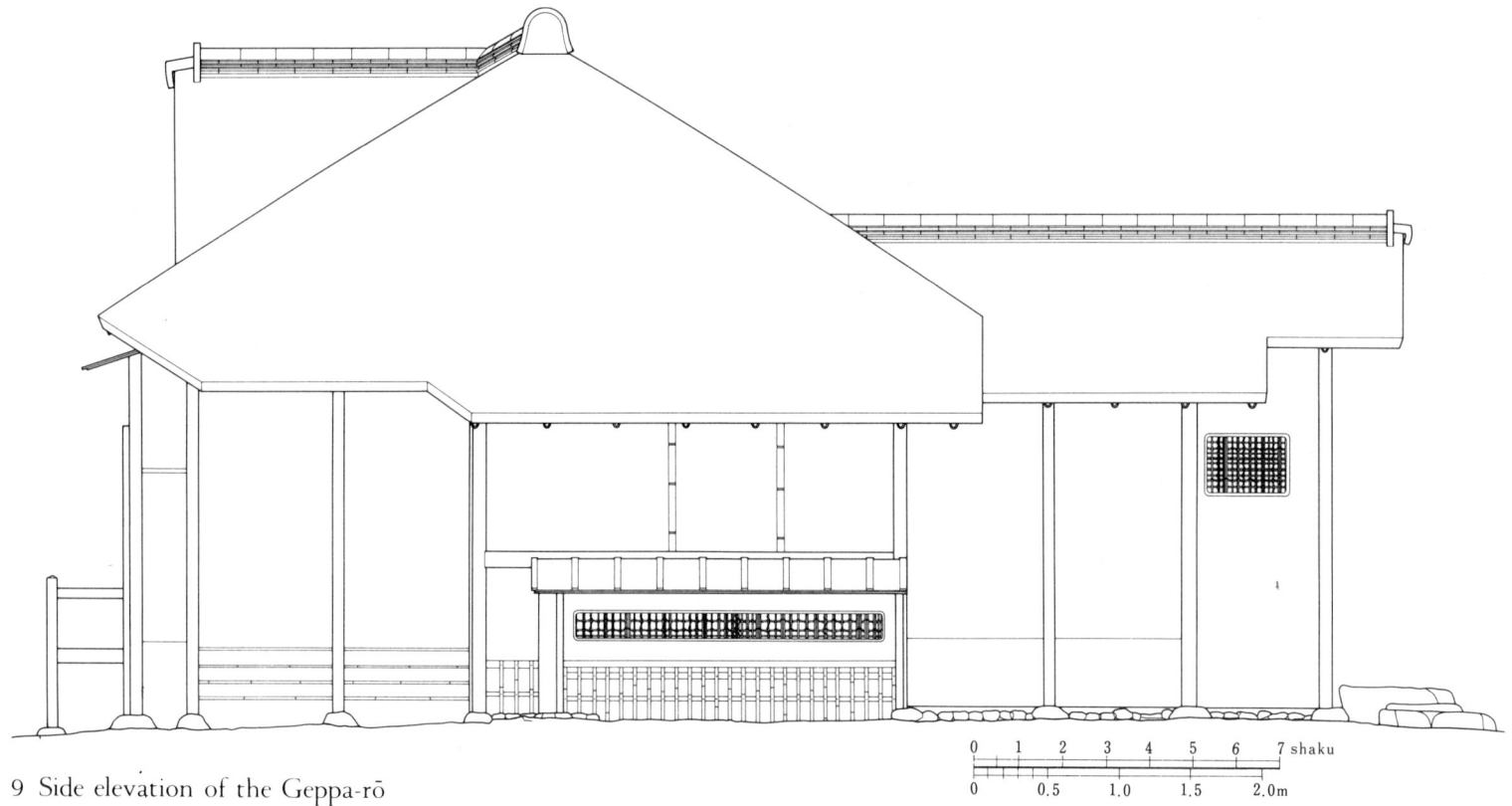

9 Side elevation of the Geppa-rō

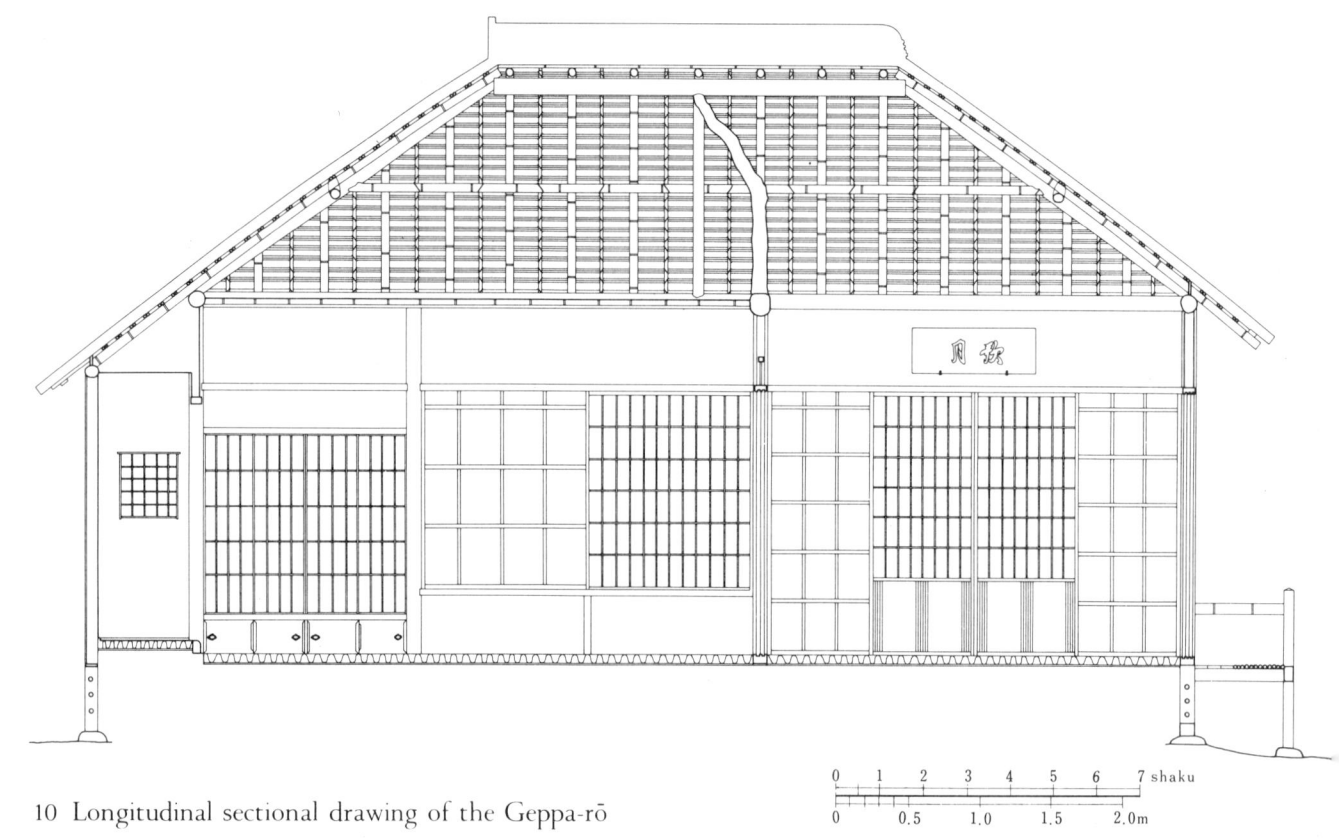

10 Longitudinal sectional drawing of the Geppa-rō

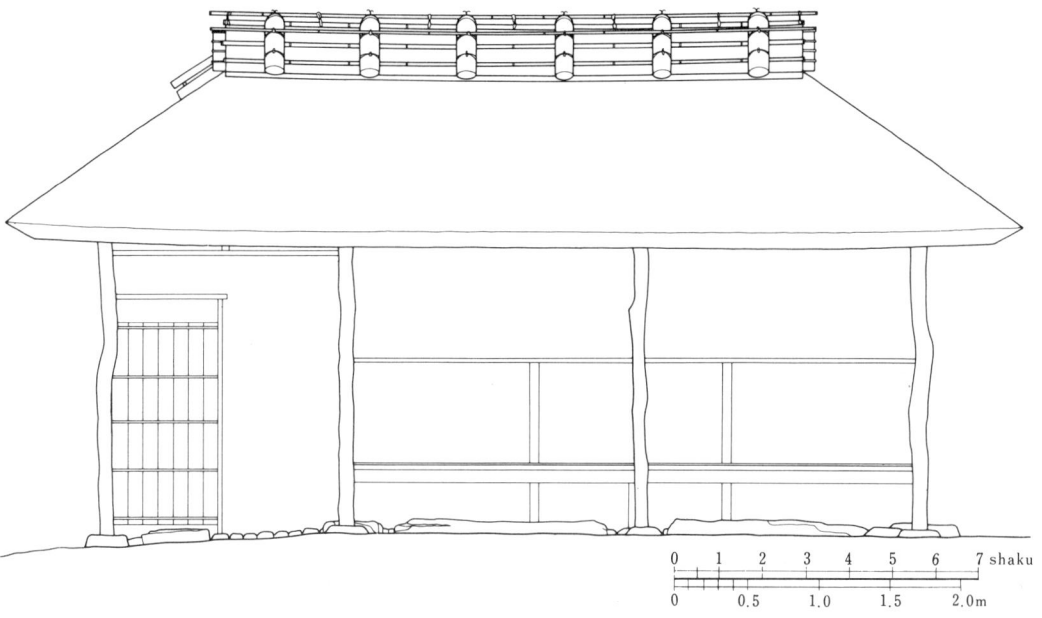

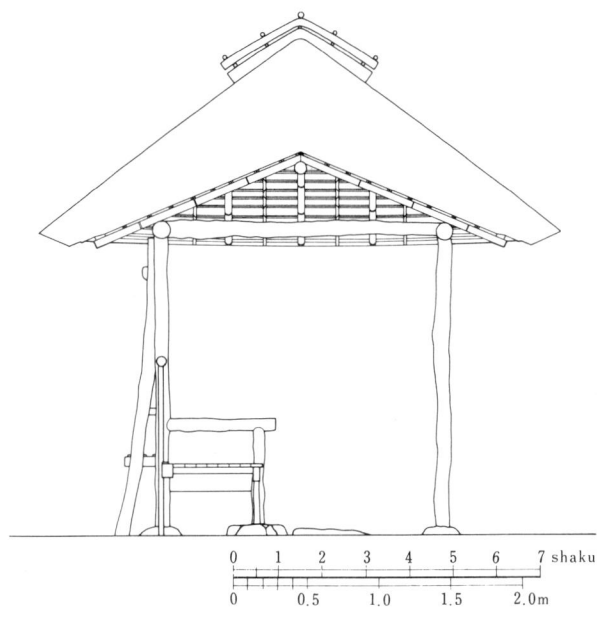

11 Front elevation of the Outer Arbor

12 Transverse sectional drawing of the Outer Arbor

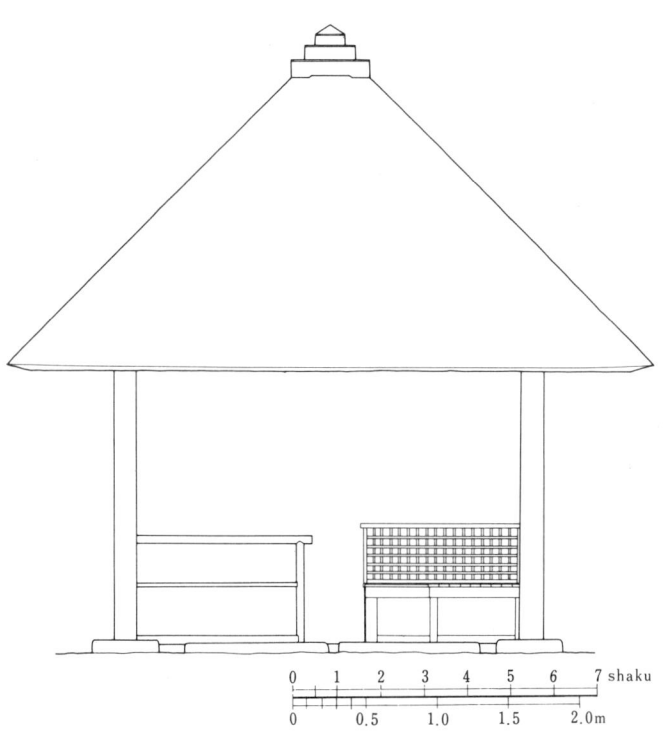

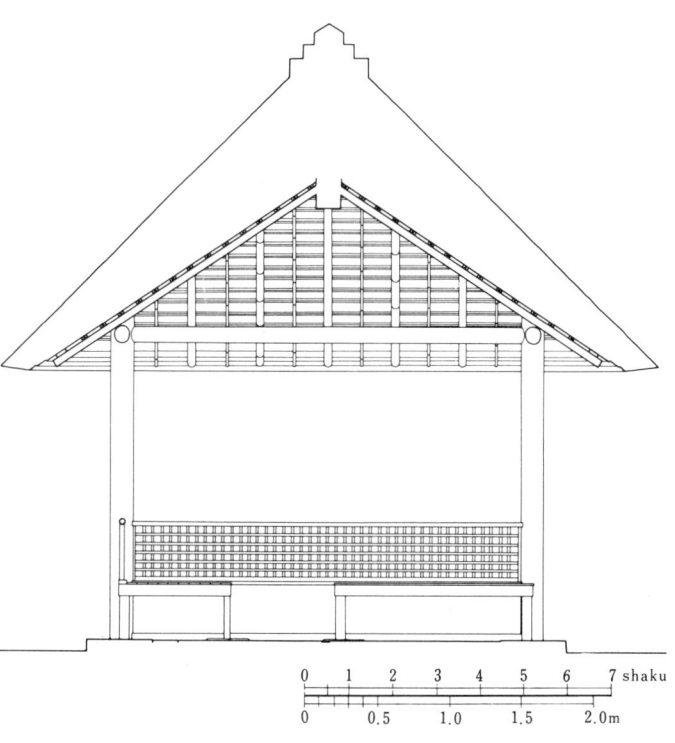

13 Front elevation of the Arbor for Four

14 Transverse sectional drawing of the Arbor for Four

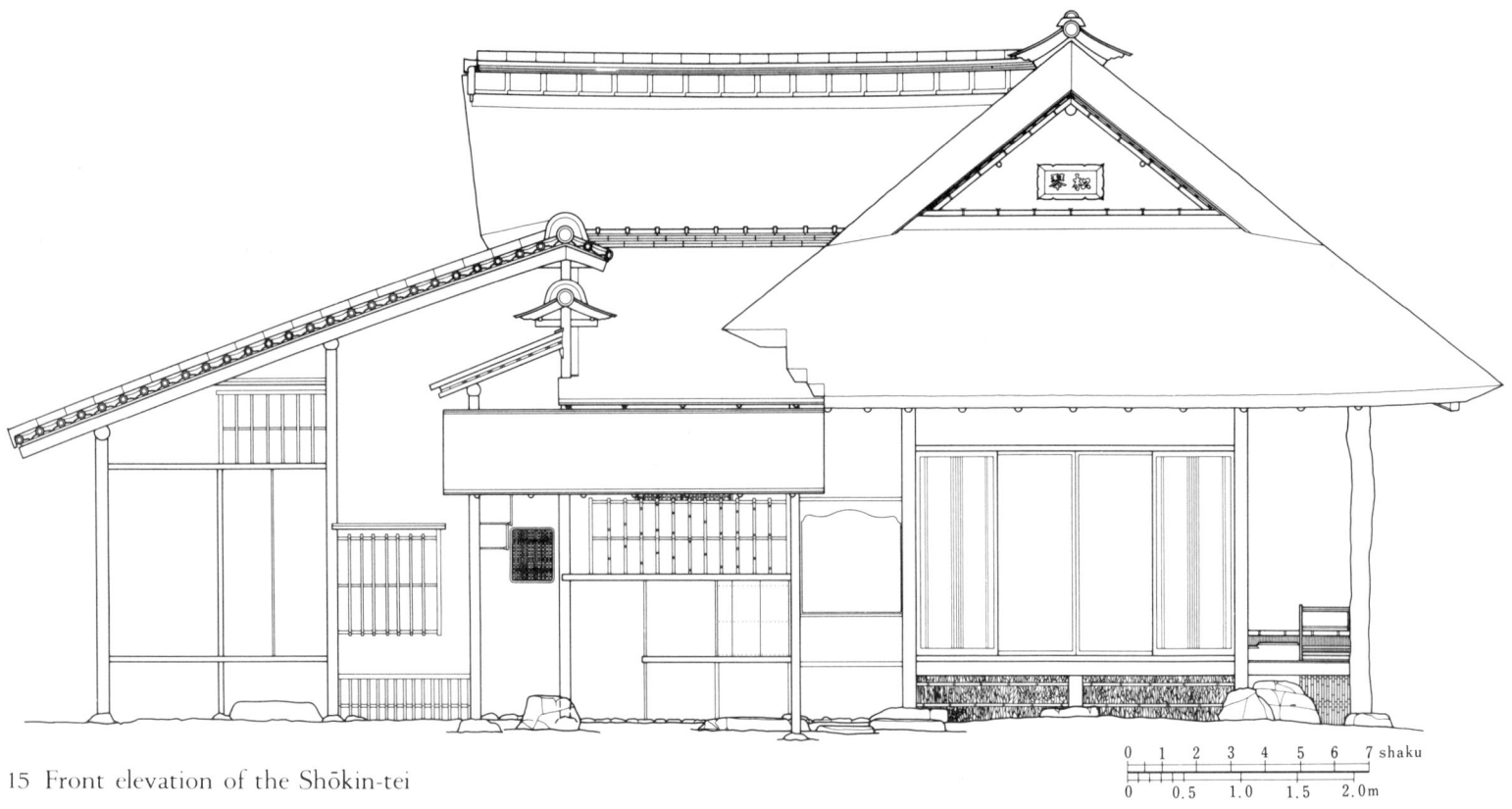

15 Front elevation of the Shōkin-tei

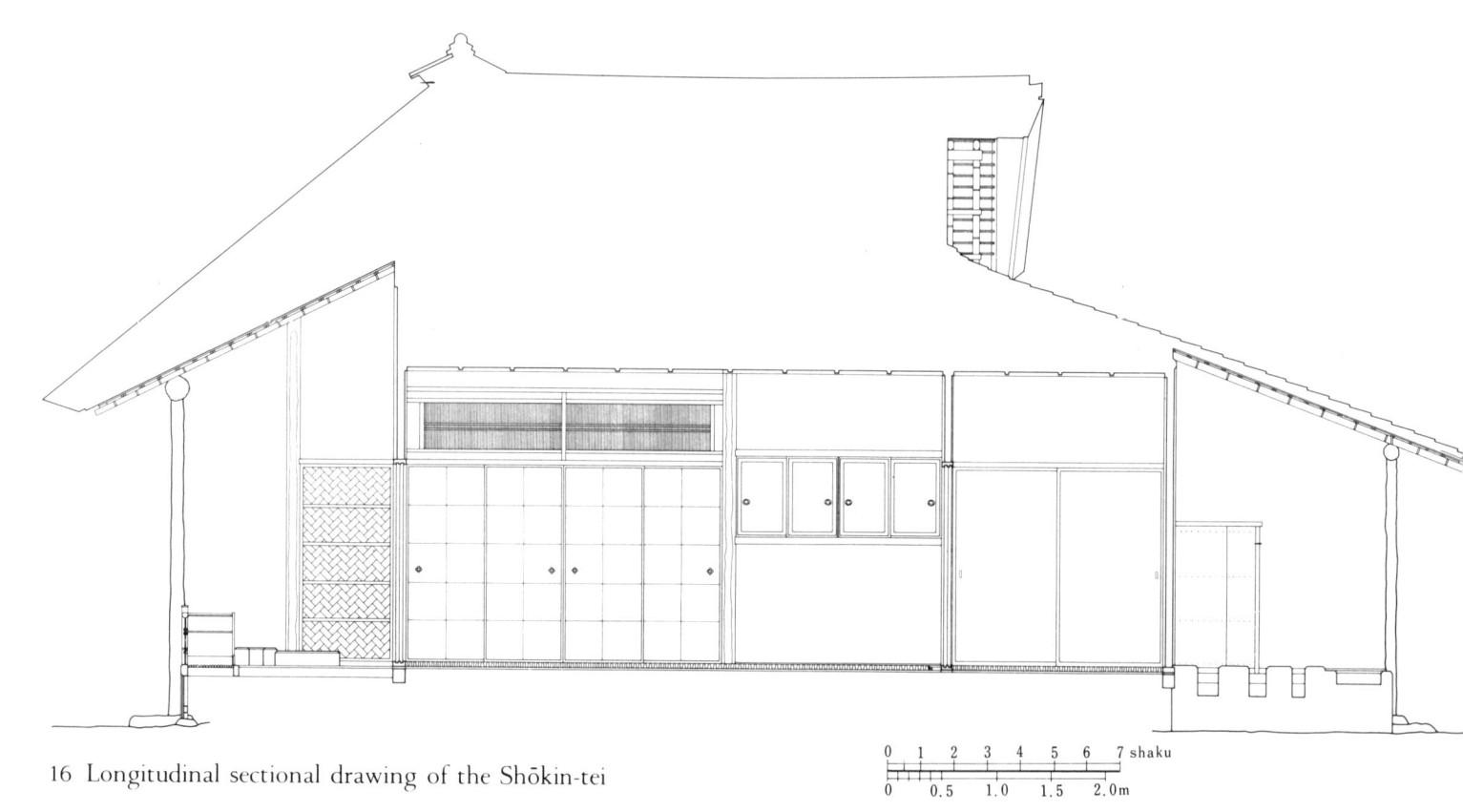

16 Longitudinal sectional drawing of the Shōkin-tei

17 Side elevation of the Shōkin-tei

0 1 2 3 4 5 6 7 shaku
0 0.5 1.0 1.5 2.0m

18 Transverse sectional drawing of the Shōkin-tei

0 1 2 3 4 5 6 7 shaku
0 0.5 1.0 1.5 2.0m

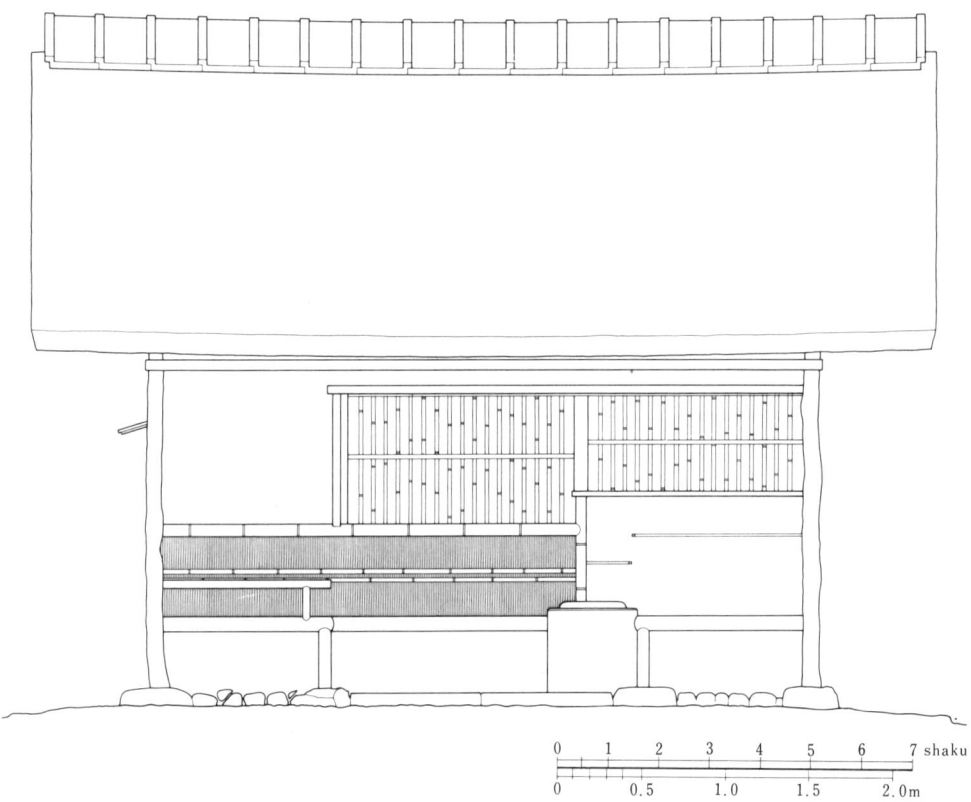

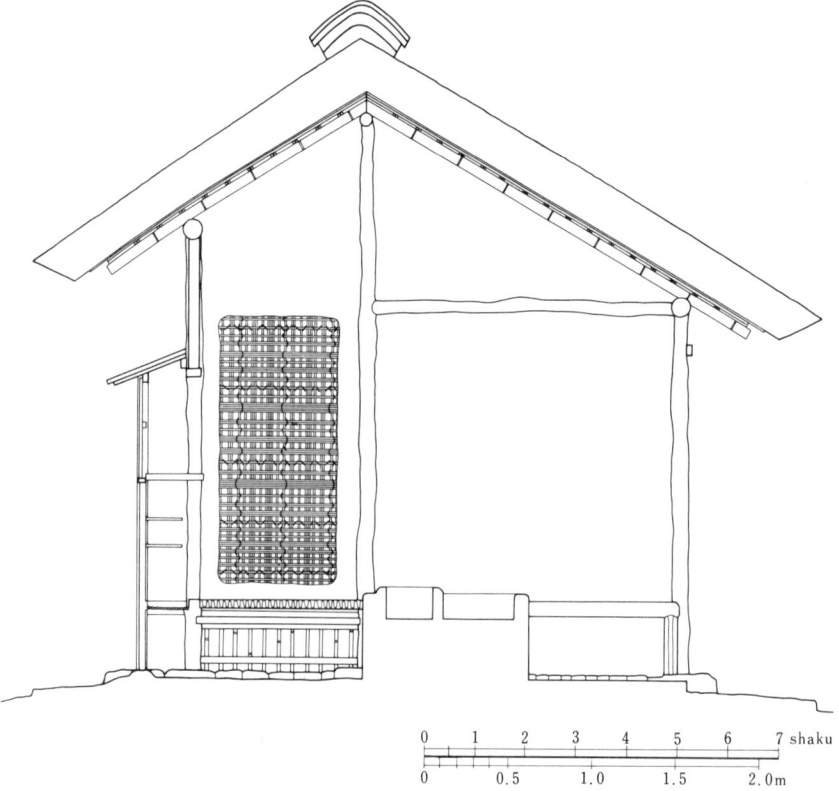

19 Front elevation of the Shōka-tei

20 Transverse sectional drawing of the Shōka-tei

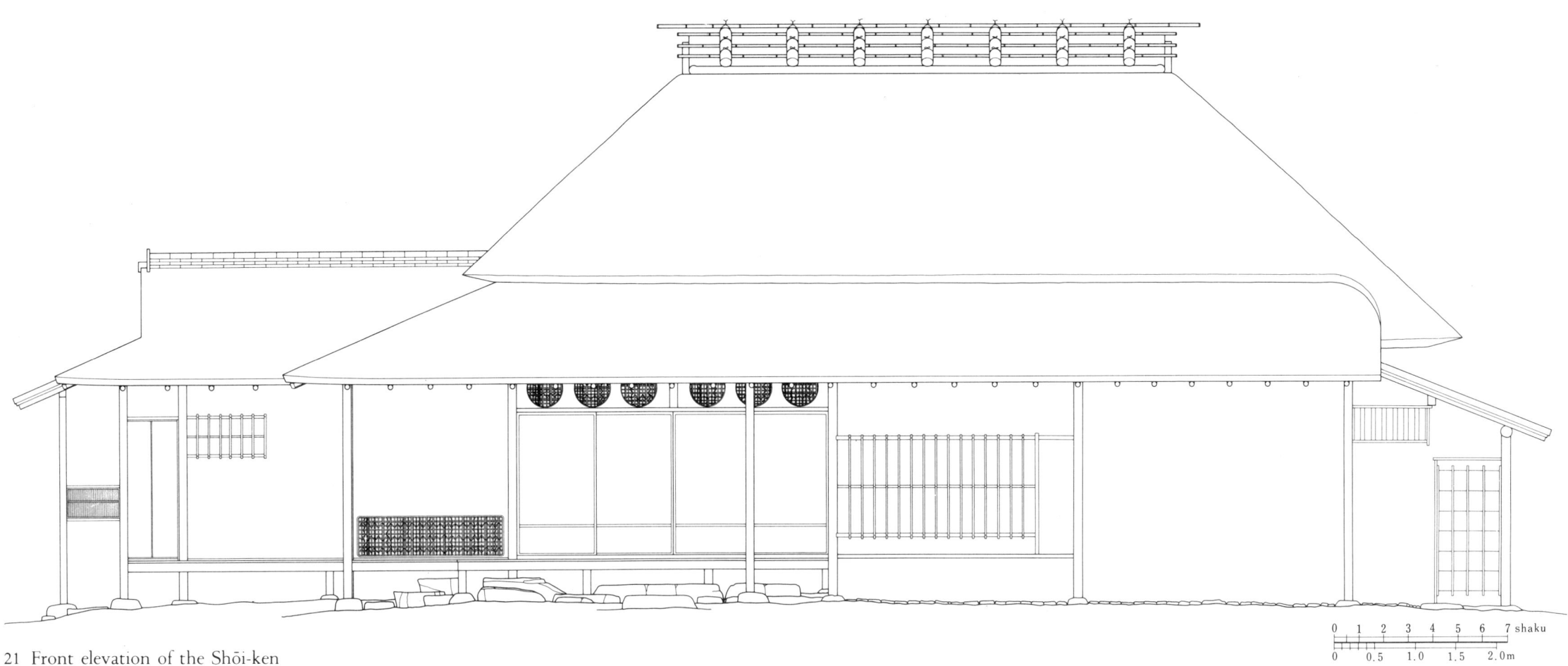

21 Front elevation of the Shōi-ken

0 1 2 3 4 5 6 7 shaku
0   0.5   1.0   1.5   2.0m

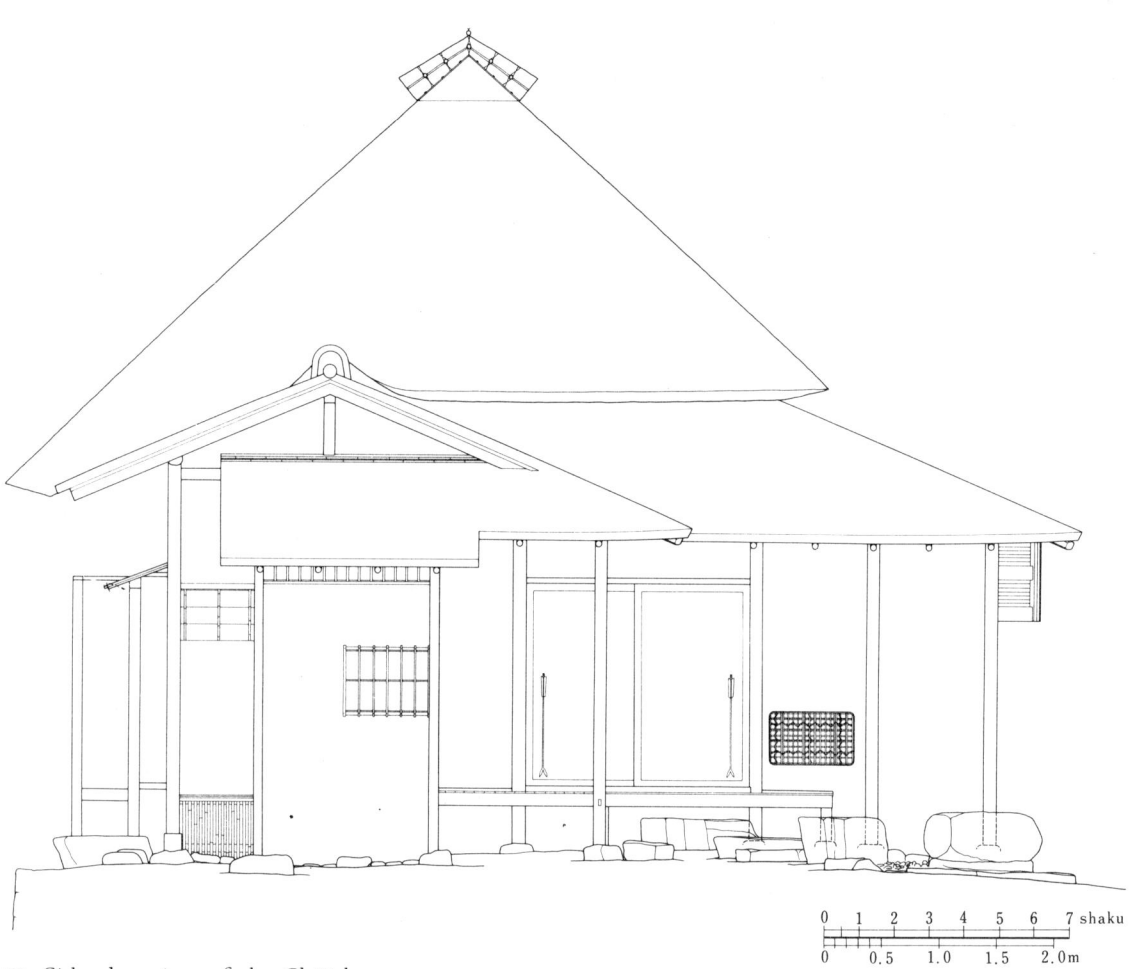

22 Side elevation of the Shōi-ken

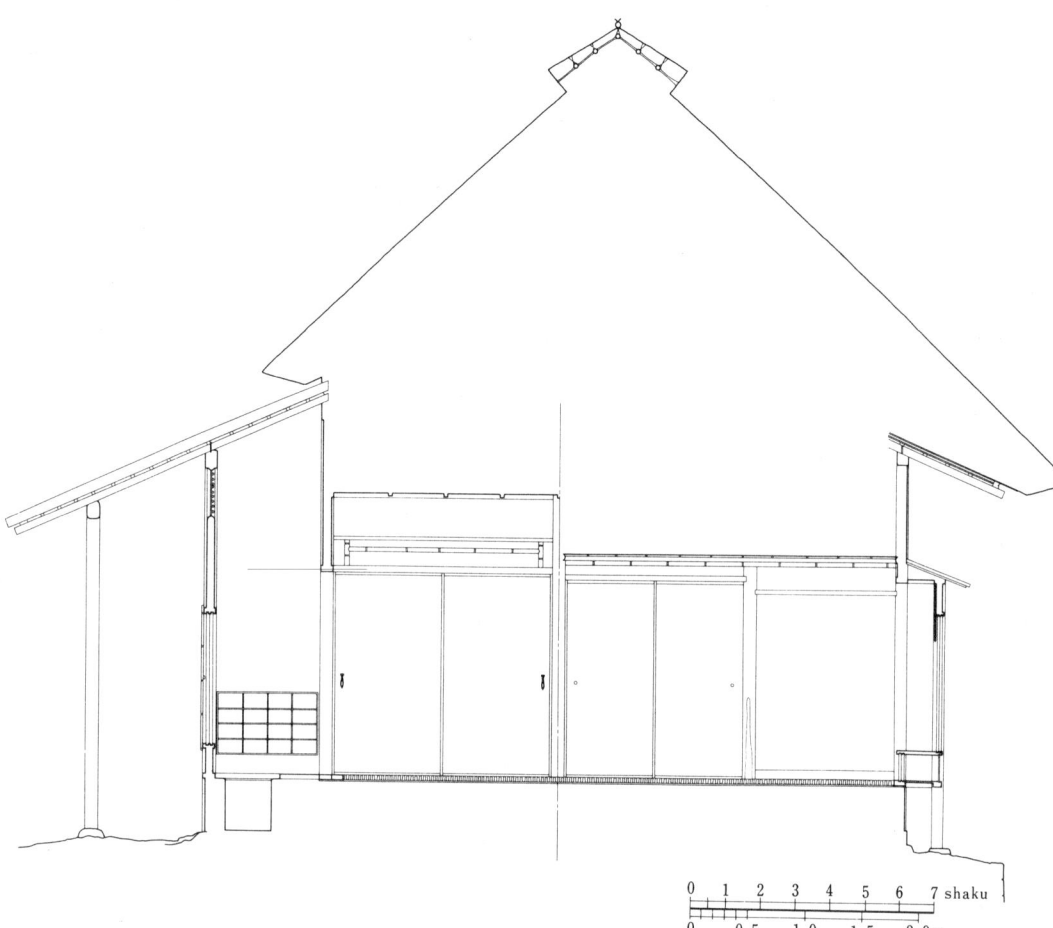

23 Transverse sectional drawing of the Shōi-ken

SELECTED BIBLIOGRAPHY

English

Gropius, Walter; Tange, Kenzō; and Ishimoto, Yasuhiro. *Katsura: Tradition and Creation in Japanese Architecture*. New Haven: Yale University Press, 1960; and Tokyo: Zokeisha, 1960.

Ōkawa, Naomi. *Edo Architecture: Katsura and Nikko*. New York and Tokyo: Weatherhill, 1975.

Japanese

Fujioka, Michio. *Katsura Rikyū* (*The Katsura Detached Palace*). Tokyo: Chūō Kōron Bijutsu Shuppansha, 1965.

Hisatsune, Shūji. *Katsura Gosho* (*The Katsura Imperial Palace*). Tokyo: Shin-chōsha, 1962.

Horiguchi, Sutemi. *Katsura Rikyū* (*The Katsura Detached Palace*). Tokyo: Mainichi Shimbunsha, 1952.

Itō, Teiji. "Kuruizaki no Katsura Rikyū" ("Katsura Palace: A Blossom Out of Season"). *Shinkenchiku*, vol. 31, no. 11 (1956).

Kawakami, Kunimoto. *Katsura Rikyū Goshashin oyobi Jissokuzu* (*Photographs and Survey Drawings of the Katsura Detached Palace*). Kokenchiku oyobi Teien Kenkyūkai (Society for Research on Old Architecture and Gardens), 1932.

Kawakami, Mitsugu, and Nakamura, Masao. *Katsura Rikyū to Chashitsu* (*The Katsura Detached Palace and Teahouse Architecture*), *Genshoku Nihon no Bijutsu* (*The Art of Japan in Color*), vol. 15. Tokyo: Shōgakkan, 1967.

Mori, Osamu. "Katsura Gobetsugyō-no-ki ni tsuite" ("Concerning the *Record of the Country House at Katsura*"). *Kenchikushi*, vol. 4, no. 5 (1942).

—————. *Katsura Rikyū* (*The Katsura Detached Palace*). Tokyo: Sōgensha, 1950.

—————. *Katsura Rikyū* (*The Katsura Detached Palace*). Tokyo: Tōto Bunka Shuppansha, 1955.

—————. *Katsura Rikyū* (*The Katsura Detached Palace*). Tokyo: Mainichi Shimbunsha, 1970.

Naitō, Akira. *Shin Katsura Rikyūron* (*New Theory Concerning the Katsura Detached Palace*). Tokyo: Kajima Shuppansha, 1967.

Sawajima, Eitarō. *Katsura Gosansō* (*The Katsura Country House*). *Tōa Kenchiku Sensho* (*Selected Books on East Asian Architecture*). Ryūginsha, 1944.

Taut, Bruno. *Nihonbi no Saihakken: Kenchikugaku-teki Kōsatsu* (*Rediscovery of Japanese Beauty: An Architectural Consideration*), translation of an unpublished work in German. Tokyo: Iwanami Shoten, 1939.

—————. *Nippon: Katsura Rikyū* (*Japan: The Katsura Detached Palace*), translation of an unpublished work in German. Tokyo: Meiji Shoin, 1934.

Toyama, Eisaku. "Katsura Rikyū no Dentō-teki Teienron o Haisu" ("Refutation of Traditional Theories Concerning the Katsura Palace Garden"). *Kokka*, vol. 37, no. 11 through vol. 38, no. 3 (1927–28).

Watsuji, Tetsurō. *Katsura Rikyū: Yoshiki no Haigo o Saguru* (*The Katsura Detached Palace: Research into the Background of Its Style*). Tokyo: Chūō Kōronsha, 1958.

Note: Translations of the Japanese titles are provided for the reader's convenience only. The English titles do not necessarily appear on the publications in question, either in the form given here or in any other.

INDEX

Boldface indicates color plate numbers.

定価15,000円
in Japan